W9-CCC-596

WHO IS THIS JESUS?

WHO IS THIS JESUS?

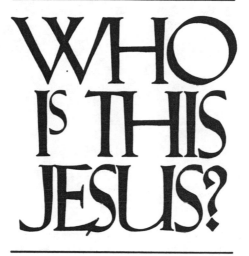

MICHAEL GREEN

OLIVER
NELSON

A Division of Thomas Nelson Publishers
Nashville

Published in Nashville, Tennessee, by Oliver-Nelson Books, a division of Thomas Nelson, Inc., Publishers, and distributed in Canada by Lawson Falle, Ltd., Cambridge, Ontario.

First published in Great Britain 1991 by Hodder and Stoughton Limited of Mill Road, Dunton Green, Sevenoaks, Kent, TN13 2YA, England. Original title: WHO IS THIS JESUS?

The Bible version used in this publication is the Revised Standard Version of the Bible, copyrighted 1946, 1952, © 1971, 1973.

Printed in the United States of America.

ISBN 0-8407-9158-5

2 3 4 5 6 — 97 96 95 94 93 92

Contents

Author's Preface   ix
1. Who Is This Jesus?   1
2. What Was He Like?   8
3. Where Did It All Start?   16
4. What Did He Teach?   28
5. What Did He Do?   39
6. What Did He Claim?   50
7. Why Did He Die?   63
8. Was Death the End?   76
9. Can We Meet Him?   88
10. What About the Church?   98

Footnotes for the Curious:
11. Jesus: What Is the Secular Evidence?   113
12. Jesus: Can We Trust the Gospels?   122

Author's Preface

The decade A.D. 1990–2000 has been designated by many denominations, including the Roman Catholic, the Lutheran, and the Anglican, as ten years when the church is going to pay particular attention to spreading the good news of Jesus among those who do not know Him — "evangelism" as it is more technically called. I have just written a substantial book on that subject called *Evangelism Through the Local Church*. Two publishers independently approached me and asked if I would follow that with a short, simple, and utterly nontechnical book about Jesus. This would serve as a tool during the decade of evangelism. It would be something about Jesus to put into the hands of open-minded inquirers.

So I decided to try during the sabbatical term that Regent College has generously given me. It has not been easy for a New Testament teacher to write that kind of book. There is the temptation, on the one hand, to justify all statements and cite all biblical references, which would have killed the book. There is the danger, on the other hand, of making too many assumptions in what is, in many parts of the West, a post-Christian society. But I have made the attempt. And I offer it in the hope that it may bring Jesus into focus for those to whom He is something of a blur. If this book helps some people to that life-changing encounter with Jesus, which lies at the heart of authentic

Christianity, I shall be overjoyed. Meanwhile I want to thank David Wavre, Carolyn Armitage, Lyn McLelland, Kim Cross, and Jane Holloway who have read it carefully and made very helpful improvements.

CHAPTER ONE

~

Who Is This Jesus?

Jesus Christ! Today these words are most frequently used as swear words. We utter them in order to vent our anger or frustration. Fifty years ago it would have been seen as blasphemy to use His name that way. But now it is commonplace. Isn't it remarkable that the name of the Man who founded the world's largest religion should be most familiar as a term of abuse? That does not happen to Muhammad or Buddha, or, for that matter, to Lenin or Mao.

Modern people in the West are embarrassed about Jesus. It is not fashionable to talk about Him. To mention His name at a party is a sure conversation-stopper. That does not happen with the other leaders of the world's religions. Nobody is embarrassed to talk about them.

But we could go farther. There is something in us that is deeply hostile to Jesus. You have only to go to a party and start talking about Him. The reaction will be immediate. You will be made to feel very uncomfortable to say the least. You may even be shouted down. But you could talk about Gandhi or the Dalai Lama to your heart's content. At worst you might seem a bid odd.

Had Jesus been a bad Man, had He been truculent and vindictive, had He been a mass murderer or a Don Juan, such reactions would be easy to understand. But He was nothing of the kind. He was the most dynamic, attractive, and genuinely good human being who ever lived.

An anonymous writer has captured the heart of the matter brilliantly in a little piece called *One Solitary Life*. It runs like this:

He was born in an obscure village, the child of a peasant woman.

He grew up in still another village, where he worked in a carpenter's shop until he was thirty. Then for three years he was an itinerant preacher.

He never wrote a book. He never held an office. He never had a family or owned a house. He did not go to college. He never visited a big city. He never travelled two hundred miles from the place where he was born. He did none of the things one usually associates with greatness.

He had no credentials but himself.

He was only thirty-three when the tide of public opinion turned against him. His friends ran away. He was turned over to his enemies and went through the mockery of a trial. He was nailed to a cross between two thieves. While he was dying, his executioners gambled for his clothing, the only property he had on earth. When he was dead, he was laid in a borrowed grave through the pity of a friend.

Nineteen centuries have come and gone, and today he remains the central figure of the human race, and the leader of mankind's progress. All the armies that ever marched, all the navies that ever sailed, all parliaments that ever sat, all the kings that ever reigned, *put together*, have not affected the life of man on this planet so much as that one solitary life.

His Impact

Strong words but hard to deny. I write in a year when Eastern Europe has been transformed beyond recognition and in ways nobody could have predicted. The causes are no doubt complex, but high among them is the lasting impact of Jesus. The longing for justice in Eastern Europe has been fueled by that "one solitary life." In Russia, religious faith has survived nearly seventy years of determined assault by militant atheism and now numbers at least sixty million Christians, many of whom, like Alexander Solzhenitsyn, have been tempered by imprisonment in gulags and mental hospitals for their beliefs. Such people have been at the heart of the reform movement that has eventually flowered in *perestroika* and *glasnost*. In Poland, Solidarity began, and largely continues, as a nonviolent Christian rebellion against an authoritarianism that crippled the human spirit. It is around the church that popular support has rallied in the independence movements of Lithuania, Latvia, and Georgia; and it is the church that has sustained their spirits amid the sea of atheism and political oppression. It was a Romanian pastor who ignited the flame of his country's uprising against the dictator's ruthless regime. The prayer meetings in Leipzig lighted the fuse that exploded in East Germany's peaceful revolution. We could not ask for clearer evidence of the impact of Jesus. That one solitary life continues to have an unparalleled impact on human affairs.

If we turn from the political to the social scene, His influence is just as obvious. For love of Jesus, Fr. Damien founded a hospice on the Hawaiian island of Molokai to serve the lepers exiled there without homes, food, or medicine. He tended them and bound up their sores until he himself contracted leprosy and died. For love of Jesus, Mother Teresa's Sisters of Mercy are caring for terminally ill AIDS patients in many countries. For love of Jesus, Charles Colson, former presidential aide at the White House, has thrown his whole life into serving the prisoners in U.S. penitentiaries, while David Wilkerson, converted from a life of crime, has created the most effective drug rehabilitation service in the world. For love of Jesus, Jackie Pullinger has given her life to the dregs of Hong Kong society, notably in the slum of the Walled City where every possible vice has flourished and police have been afraid to enter. A flourishing Christian community has grown out of this loving commitment to the poor and unlovely. Would attachment to any of the other great religious leaders of the world have inspired such dedication and self-sacrifice? There must be something very special about this Jesus. And yet we do not want to know.

Our Reluctance

That becomes the more amazing the longer you think about it. Fancy not wanting to know about the one solitary life that has affected this world more than any other! Just suppose we were invited to meet a close associate of one of the great athletes of the world, a distinguished statesman, a famous actor, or a brilliant scientist. I have no doubt what our reaction would be. We would be keen to meet such a person, and we would feel privileged to find out from the inside as much as we could about the public hero we admired. Why, then, do we shy away from Jesus? Why are we embarrassed, antagonistic even, when someone wants to talk to us about Him? There is something very strange here. Plato maintained that humankind can't help but love the highest when he sees it. Plato was wrong. The highest example of what it means to be human lies before us in Jesus Christ. His story is superbly recounted in the four Gospels. But although the Bible that contains them is the world's best-seller, it has been called "the book nobody knows." And although its central figure, Jesus Christ, is the most influential person in the history of the world, He could aptly be called "the Man nobody knows."

Why are we so reluctant to take a fresh look at Jesus?

Is it because of the church? The society Jesus founded has been so unlike Jesus. Think of the bloodthirsty Crusades, the cruel Inquisition, and the history of religious persecution. The church is still so unlike Jesus, and we may well have been scarred by its hypocrisy or bored by its blandness. We recall, maybe, that dreary local church to which we were dragged, protesting, when we were young. Or we reflect on the divisions of the church, the failures of its leadership, and the small difference it seems to make to the lives of its members. Is that why we don't want to know about Jesus?

Or is it because the very brightness of Jesus' life shows up the dark corners of our own? We do not want to get too close to Him because we have a nasty suspicion that He would expect some major changes in our lifestyle? Jesus Himself recognized that we love darkness rather than light because our deeds are evil, and will not come to the light in case those deeds should be exposed (see John 3:19–20).

Or is it, perhaps, because the very name of Jesus has uncomfortable overtones of deity about it, which pose a threat to our own heady ideas of freedom and human potential? Does the name of Jesus remind us of two thoughts we most want to suppress, our mortality and our accountability? We shall have to die one day. What if death is not the end? What if we have to face the God who gave us our freedom and our potential? That is a most disagreeable possibility. We don't want to consider it.

All three of these reasons may be partial explanations of our reluctance to take a closer look at Jesus, the Jesus we threw out as children — along with Santa Claus. But since something like one-third of humankind maintains that this same Jesus Christ is alive today, that His friendship is open to all, life-changing, and utterly fulfilling — well, we might be wise to think again. The churches may have obscured Jesus as well as revealed Him; but nobody rejects electricity because some of the substations break down. We may feel embarrassed at the perfection of Jesus; but any changes He may advocate for our lives are only changes for the better. And the name of Jesus may challenge us about the ultimate issues of life and death; but those issues have to be faced. Indeed, He may turn out to hold the key to them.

The Invitation

So why should we not take it further and examine the person of Jesus afresh, with an open mind? We shall not be wasting our time. The character of Jesus is immensely attractive. It embodies all that we ourselves would, in our best moments, like to be. The teachings of Jesus are without doubt the greatest that have ever been offered to humankind. The death of Jesus is certainly the most famous in the history of the world. And the claims of Jesus are so startling that they stop us in our tracks and challenge us to make up our minds about this most remarkable person. Was He just a great teacher? Or was He much more?

There are, I think, two reasons that make an investigation of Jesus Christ particularly significant in this last decade of the century. The first is that, for all our scientific and technological advances, human nature has changed very little. A candid look at our world reveals much violence and hatred, much cruelty and lust, much fouling of our cosmic nest and indifference to the plight of fellow human beings. Starvation and greed, corruption and strife — be it at family, societal, or international levels — remain dangerous threats to our survival as a race. And all the time the human heart cries out for love and forgiveness, for meaning and reconciliation, for peace and hope. These are the very issues that Jesus spent His life addressing. His followers maintain that He addresses them still.

The second reason why we should examine Jesus Christ afresh is that many people know so little about Him these days. You hear nothing of Him in the workplace, nothing much in schools or universities, nothing in most homes. Even many churches seem to speak of everything but Jesus Christ. In any case, churchgoing is now, in the West, a minority interest. So where can we find out about Jesus? Where is there a clear, succinct account of what we know about Him, who He was and what He achieved, why His followers worship Him, and what relevance He can have for our lives and society? There are a few books that help but very few. I am going to take the risk of adding one more in the hope that it will, for some, dispel clouds of ignorance and misunderstanding and enable them to make up their own minds about the greatest person who ever lived.

CHAPTER TWO

~

What Was He Like?

A very fair question. But how impossibly difficult to answer!

One thing, though, is certain. The Jesus who meets us in the pages of the four Gospels (the accounts of Jesus written by His friends — see chapter 12) is very different from the picture many have of Him. He is nothing like the "gentle Jesus meek and mild" of the children's stories. He is not the miserable holy man who never laughs. He is not the fearsome judge who watches to see if we are enjoying ourselves and then tells us to stop. Nor is He the lifeless figure in the stained-glass window. Jesus, as the Gospels reveal Him to us, is radiantly alive and supremely attractive.

There is a great deal we would love to know that we simply are not told. We do not even know what He looked like. He was a Palestinian Jew, and as such the color of His skin would be olive, His eyes brown, and His nose hooked. Palestinian Jews had black hair and usually wore it long and carefully groomed. They valued a full beard, and it appears on many of the coins of the day. His mother tongue was Aramaic, a dialect of Hebrew, which He would have spoken with a northern accent common to Galilee where He was brought up. But He could speak Greek and probably some Latin and was thoroughly at home in the Hebrew Scriptures. He wore a sleeveless undergarment with a girdle, the customary cloak and sandals, and carried a staff on journeys. That is all we know about His appearance or can guess with confidence.

But the Gospels have no interest in these things. They are profoundly disinterested in His size, the color of His eyes and hair, and even His age and strength. These external things are unimportant. What a man is like stems from his character. And here the Gospels are eloquent.

He Was Great Company

The first thing that strikes me is that Jesus was such delightful company. People walked miles to be with Him. And they were folk from widely different backgrounds who normally would have had nothing in common. Judges and soldiers, fishermen and prostitutes — all found His company irresistible. He cheerfully broke the taboos that kept people apart in Judaism's highly structured society. He mixed with top people and street people with equal ease. He was at home in the tavern just as He was in the temple. He could win the adoration of the crowd, yet loved solitary and simple settings.

He was an inspiration to the uneducated and intellectuals alike. Although Himself a carpenter, devoid of theological training, He could attract and teach a man like Nicodemus who had the highest theological training and social privileges in the nation. He could also offer an entirely new life to a wildly immoral woman from a hostile neighboring country. Indeed, women were welcomed as an important part of His movement: He respected them, and they were devoted to Him. This was most remarkable in a culture where the pious Jew thanked God daily that he was not born a woman. Jesus was sometimes to be found surrounded by little children, bouncing delightedly upon His knee. He held them up as examples to grown men and women whereas normal religious leaders were too solemn and self-important to view them as anything but an intrusion. Jesus was a Man for all types. He was marvelous company.

He Made God Real

The second thing I notice is that He was intensely aware of God. To Him, God was not some absentee world ruler but His Father (He even called Him "Daddy") with whom He was in constant touch. We often read of His disappearing for a time of prayer, particularly when about to make some important decision. We hear His astonishing claim, "I do nothing but what I see the Father do." We hear Him say, quite unself-consciously, "I do always those things that please Him." The way He made God so real, the way He brought Him into the heart of everyday affairs often puzzled His hearers. He claimed that He and His Father were one. Not literally, of course. But Jesus meant that He lived so close to His unseen yet intensely real heavenly Father that He provided an unclouded window into God. That was the claim; and the way Jesus lived and prayed, talked and acted, substantiated it. Many who met Jesus felt they had come into contact with God. And they loved it. The God that Jesus embodied was so attractive, so fair, so loving, so altogether beautiful that they found themselves not embarrassed and alienated but attracted to Him. Jesus had made God truly accessible for the first time in their lives.

His Life Was Matchless

The third thing that comes before us in the gospel account is the sheer quality of His life. If you were looking for perfection, you would need to look no further. The life of Jesus shines out as the ideal for all humanity.

There is no vice that shows up in His character. There is no virtue that He did not have. We read of His getting exhausted in the service of others but never of His turning them away. We see Him parched by the heat of the sun but not too thirsty to converse with a needy woman and to help her. We find Him weeping at the tomb of His friend Lazarus, in sympathy for the family and in affection for the dead man. We find Him touching the eyes of a blind man and restoring vision, or laying His hands on a leper, fearless of the grim disease, and restoring him to health. His great compassion for people in any kind of need is very attractive. That compassion flowed out to the sick child of a nobleman, to a lonely tax collector (alienated from everybody by his rapacious greed), and even to the soldiers who nailed Him to the cross. Politically nonaligned, He numbered the conventional conservative like Nicodemus, the Roman collaborator like Matthew, and the revolutionary freedom fighter like Simon the Zealot among His followers. He was at home in any company. His joy, His vitality, His passionate uprightness, His constant outgoing care, and the power that attended both His teaching and His actions — all made virtue front page news.

He described the love of God as being like a woman searching for one lost coin or a shepherd tracking down one lost sheep. That is how much every individual in the world matters to God, He maintained. And that is how much each individual mattered to Jesus. There has never been such an example of unselfish love, tirelessly poured out for others. His has proved an impossible act for anyone to follow. Perhaps He really is the ideal for humankind?

His Teaching Was Authoritative

The sheer authority of Jesus jumps at us out of the pages of the Gospels. The reaction we find in Mark's gospel after Jesus' first address was this: "They were astonished at his teaching, for he taught them as one who had authority, and not as the scribes" (Mark 1:22). The scribes were the clergy of the day. They, like modern scholars, constantly appealed to others as authorities. But in Jesus you find no footnotes. He never quotes the opinions of other teachers from the past, except the prophets. Instead, He coins a phrase that carries its own authority: "Truly, truly I tell you." Here is a Man who did not speculate about the things of God. He knew. And people recognized it.

His Actions Spelled Power

But it was not only the power of His teaching that struck people so forcefully. It was the authority of His deeds. Who was this young carpenter who could walk into the temple and challenge the high priest's domain by breaking up the crooked market that had developed there and by sending the traders packing? Who was this who could say to a paralyzed man, "Stretch out your hand," and immediately restore it to health? Who was this who could drive out the dark forces that were ruining a man's life and making him gash himself with knives as he eked out a shadowy, tormented existence among the tombs? Who was this who could address a storm as if it were a living thing and bid it cease its raging? Who was this who could tell His disciples with cool confidence to go and feed five thousand people with five little buns and a few local fish? Who was this who could face the Roman governor, the man who thought he had the power of life and death over Jesus, and calmly say that he could have no power over Him whatsoever unless it was allowed him by His heavenly Father? What a Man! What simply staggering authority!

His Freedom Was Complete

Another feature of Jesus' character that dances on the pages of the Gospels is His freedom. Was there ever anyone so free? Born into a working-class family, He was entirely free of social prejudice. Although He was a member of a subject race under Roman occupation, He appeared to be in complete control of His circumstances. He was a strong believer in the Old Testament, and yet He felt free to reinterpret its general precepts in particular cases. He was no slave to the system. He was the liberator. He freed people from guilt and from a low self-image. He healed them of the spiritual sickness that ravaged their character and the physical illness that marred their health. He released people from fear simply by His presence alongside them. Often we find Him saying, "Fear not. It is I. Do not be afraid."

Free from fear, He was also free from arrogance. He had no taboos, no chips on the shoulder, no pride, no mealymouthed humility. What a free Man! He never drew a sword or cast a vote, yet His teaching has been one of the most potent weapons for reforming community and personal life worldwide ever since. He never freed a slave or enfranchised a woman, yet His attitudes and teaching were the inspiration of the great social reforms in the West that righted both these injustices. He never functioned outside Palestine, yet His precepts and His attitudes to men and women of other faiths and other races have led to the worldwide missionary movement and to the breakdown of color and class prejudice. He was free to hold on to His life and feather His nest, had He so chosen. But He did not.

Instead He died at the age of thirty-three. Why? Not because the big battalions caught up with Him at last, or because He had become enmeshed in a net from which He could not escape. But because, as we shall see in a later chapter, He was carrying out His own paradoxical yet intensely liberating teaching: "The man who holds on to his life will lose it. The man who is prepared to lose his life for the sake of Me and of the good news will find it" (see Matt. 10:39). In a mysterious yet evocative phrase, He said He had come "to give his life as a ransom for many" (Matt. 20:28). It was something He freely chose to do.

Think of Jesus at His trial, bound and blindfolded in that courtroom. Was He the prisoner, or were His accusers? Prisoners all of jealousy, pride, envy, greed, self-righteousness, and hate; but He was free, utterly free. He was calling the shots, not they.

In this age that values freedom almost more than anything else, Jesus confronts us as the most liberated Man who ever lived.

His Love Was Universal

There is just one quality that has universal recognition the world over, apart from freedom. It is love. And love is what you find at its most quintessential in Jesus. Not the watered-down parody of love we see in the movies, but the strong, deathless love of God Himself. Nobody taught about it like Jesus. Nobody embodied it like He. It all springs, He maintained, from the God who so loved the world that He gave His one and only Son so that those who believe in Him should not perish but have eternal life. Jesus' whole life and ministry were bathed in love, tireless, outgoing unselfish love to all and sundry. Love for His friends, those vacillating, disappointing, unreliable disciples of His: "Having loved his own who were in the world, he loved them to the end" (John 13:1). Love for the unlovely: He showed that love at every turn, be it for the rich nobleman who was trapped by his wealth and unable to face the cost of discipleship or for the beggar by the roadside crying out for help. Love for the rank bad lots in society, the swindlers, the prostitutes. Love for the outsiders, like the hated Samaritans. Love for the helpless, the blind, the children. Love for the lepers with their loathsome sores. As we have seen, He actually touched them. What crazy love! And love even for His enemies: "Father, forgive them," He cries as they drive the nails into His hands and feet on the cross (Luke 23:34).

The love Jesus taught, the love He embodies so matchlessly, was to be the supreme hallmark of His disciples. "A new commandment I give you," He said. "Love one another as I have loved you. This is how everyone will be able to tell that you are My followers: by your love for one another" (see John 13:34–35). Tragically, His followers have fallen far short of such love. But what a beacon it is, beckoning us through the night of our selfishness. And Jesus actually did love like that. Not some of the time; all of it. Not some people; but everyone. That is what Jesus was like.

CHAPTER THREE

~

Where Did It All Start?

Jesus has had an astonishing influence on the history of the world. The calendar changed with His birth. The legal system of the West owes its basis to His values. Education in many parts of the world is due to Christians who taught people to read and write so that they might find out for themselves about Jesus. Hospitals and a tremendous amount of voluntary social work and care for the poor, the sick, and the hungry go back for their inspiration to this remarkable person. So where did it all start?

There are several layers to this answer.

Roman Palestine

At the most obvious level, Jesus was born into a politically insignificant country, some 125 miles long and 50 wide, on the edge of the Roman map. It was the country of Judea, the national home of the Jewish people for many centuries. At that time the country was governed by Herod the Great, a ruthless self-serving man who was half Jew and half Gentile, and whose building exploits were matched only by his cruelty. He was not an independent ruler: he was the cat's-paw of the most powerful man in the world, Augustus Caesar. Augustus was a brilliant soldier and superb governor, who had made his position in the Roman world supreme after defeating all his rivals in 31 B.C. He chose to govern some countries on the rim of his empire by means of "client kings," using their countries to keep at bay the hordes of barbarians who were always threatening the stability of the Mediterranean world. Herod was one of these client kings. And it was in the latter days of his reign that Jesus was born. The year was 7 B.C.

This seems very strange to us. Surely Jesus should have been born in A.D. 1? The hilarious truth of the matter is that the monk who worked out all the dates some hundreds of years later got his figures wrong! Herod the Great died in 4 B.C. Jesus was born three years earlier.

The birth of Jesus caught His parents, Joseph and Mary, a little by surprise. They were not at home at the time but were registering their names and property at the place where Joseph was born, the village of Bethlehem, a few miles from the capital, Jerusalem. The Romans were anxious to get a competent taxation system going all over the empire, and this registration of names and property was the first part of the process (*aprographe*). It came to fruition a few years later with the official assessment of taxes (*apotimesis*) in A.D. 6. As a matter of fact, this was so unpopular and produced such a disturbance in the volatile land of Judea that the Romans decided to take it under their direct rule and govern it by a "procurator." They allowed the northern part of the country, Galilee, to remain under the semi-independent rule of one of Herod's sons, a man called Antipas, who figures occasionally in the gospel story. So throughout Jesus' life and ministry, Judea was an occupied country, and Roman soldiers were a common sight in Galilee as well.

The Roman occupation had profound effects not only on the daily life of the Jewish people but on the politics. It produced the Zealot movement, a fierce nationalist opposition to all things Roman. At the opposite extreme it produced the "political realists," the conservative Sadducees who were priests and landowners and had most to lose. They regretted the presence of the Romans but saw coexistence with them as the only way of survival. They held the majority in the internal government that the Romans allowed, a "sanhedrin" or council of seventy-one members, whose chairman was always the high priest.

The Pharisees constituted the third group, alongside the Zealots and the Sadducees. They figure largely in the gospel story and were very distinctive in their way of life. They did not like the Romans much but did not have the heart for taking up arms in what they were shrewd enough to know would be a hopeless struggle. So they waited for God's kingly intervention, at the time of His choosing, when the Romans would be thrown out and holy men of God (themselves) would govern the divine kingdom. Meanwhile they practiced an elaborate and ritualistic obedience both to the law that had been given long ago to the Jewish people through Moses and to the many developments that had sprung from that law during the succeeding centuries. They hoped that by so doing they would hasten the day of the Messiah, the longed-for deliverer who would rid the country of the Roman overlords and usher in a time of peace and prosperity for the nation.

The fourth group within Judaism at the time of Jesus was made up of the men who lived in the burning deserts of the south near the Dead Sea and wrote the Dead Sea Scrolls. They saw the nation as apostate, themselves as the only true believers, and the desert as the place to await the day of judgment when God would break in to throw the Romans into the sea, uproot the wicked Saducean priests, and put themselves into the leadership of the nation. They played no part in the story of Jesus in the Gospels, and they were wiped out by the Romans in A.D. 70.

Such was the little land, and such the tensions within it when

Jesus lived there at the turn of our era. Not an ideal setting for one of the greatest figures in world history! The country was seething with unrest. The government, first of Herod and then of the Romans, was heartily detested. The people were impoverished but insanely proud of their ancestry reaching back thousands of years to their founder Abraham. And although the term meant different things to different groups in society, everyone was on tiptoe of expectation that the *kingdom of God* would soon break in. Things were very dark, but then, the darkest hour always comes before the dawn.

Against this backdrop Joseph, a humble carpenter or building contractor, along with Mary, his young wife, travel to Bethlehem for the registration. When they are there, Mary's labor pains begin. What are they to do? The inns are all full. Everyone else is registering as well. It could not have happened at a worse time. But some kindly innkeeper takes pity on them and allows them access to the stable where his cattle are protected from the winter weather. It was there that Jesus was born. It was there that He was laid in a manger full of hay. That is where the story begins. And at first sight it is not a very hopeful beginning.

Ancient Prophecies

But there is another level to the story and a much earlier answer to the question, "Where did it all start?" According to the Old Testament, Abraham, the forefather of the Jewish race, had been promised by God that in his seed all the nations of the earth would be blessed (see Gen. 12:3). Much of that promise had been fulfilled in the rise, spread, and prosperity of the Jewish nation. But everyone knew there was more to come. The nation had developed a kingship that survived for many centuries. But on the whole the kings had disappointed. Even David, the most

~ 19 ~

famous of them all, had proved to be both an adulterer and a murderer. Things went from bad to worse with the royal line, until at length it was extinguished and the nation dragged off into captivity in Babylon some six hundred years before Jesus' time. But there was a word of promise from the days of the kings that was always remembered. The Lord had declared to David through the prophet Nathan:

> I will raise up your offspring after you,... and I will establish the throne of his kingdom for ever. I will be his father, and he shall be my son (2 Sam. 7:12, 13–14).

No king had ever fulfilled that prophecy. The Jewish people waited for One who would.

Then again, the prophet Isaiah, some seven hundred years before the time of Jesus, predicted,

> The Lord himself will give you a sign. Behold, a virgin shall conceive and bear a son, and shall call his name Immanuel ["God is with us"] (Isa. 7:14).

Isaiah had gone on to predict a cure for the nation's greatest need: divine forgiveness for personal and national wrongdoing. The way it was to be accomplished was awesome:

> Behold, my servant shall prosper,...
> and shall be very high.
> [He shall] startle many nations;...
> for that which has not been told them they shall see,
> and that which they have not heard they shall understand....
> He was despised and rejected by men;
> a man of sorrows, and acquainted with grief;
> and as one from whom men hide their faces
> he was despised, and we esteemed him not.

Surely he has borne our griefs
    and carried our sorrows;
yet we esteemed him stricken,
    smitten by God, and afflicted.
But he was wounded for our transgressions,
    he was bruised for our iniquities;
upon him was the chastisement that made us whole,
    and with his stripes we are healed.
All we like sheep have gone astray;
    we have turned every one to his own way;
and the LORD has laid on him
    the iniquity of us all (Isa. 52:13 — 53:7).

No one had ever fulfilled the prophecy of that wonderful child or that sinbearing servant of God. The Jewish people waited for One who would.

Those ancient prophets knew where He would come from when the time was ripe, and they knew what He would accomplish. He would be born in Bethlehem, and He would achieve nothing less than an entirely new basis for the relationship between God and man. A new "covenant," or agreement, would be struck:

You, O Bethlehem Ephrathah,
    who are little to be among the clans of Judah,
from you shall come forth...
    one who is to be ruler in Israel,
whose origin is from of old,
    from ancient days (Mic. 5:2).

This is the covenant which I will make... I will put my law within them, and I will write it upon their hearts; and I will be their God, and they shall be my people. And no longer shall each man teach his neighbor and brother, saying, "Know the LORD," for they shall all know me, from the least of them to the greatest, says the LORD; for I will forgive their iniquity, and I will remember their sin no more (Jer. 31:33–34).

What amazing insight into the very birthplace and achievements of the Liberator! And what benefits this new covenant would carry: forgiveness of sin, personal knowledge of God by all His people, and a law written on their hearts, not in a book.

Nobody had ever fulfilled those prophecies. The Jewish people waited for One who would.

It was among such speculations and hopes that Jesus was born in Bethlehem. Was it feasible to hope, perhaps, that the One who would fulfill these ancient prophecies was about to appear? Could it be that the story began not in the manger at Bethlehem's stable but centuries before in the purposes of God?

Current Conditions

Wishful thinking maybe? Perhaps. But consider. If a universal leader was ever going to emerge, there was no time in the history of the world like this. Jewish faith in one God, the source and goal of the whole universe, the creator of the moral law, had spread everywhere because of Jewish dispersion and trade. And although the Romans thought them crazy, they were secretly very jealous of their austere faith, their Holy Book, their reverent worship, and their upright lives. The Romans themselves had conquered the whole known world. Never before, and hardly ever again, had the whole of humankind been under a single ruler, and one that on the whole was just. Moreover the Romans, that most practical of people, inaugurated a better communications system than any until almost our own day. Travel was easy and safe; good news could travel fast from one end of the empire to the other. And then there was the Greek language. It was rather as English has become in our day, the common language understood and used all over the world. What with Jewish faith, Greek language, and Roman Empire, the world was uniquely ready for the coming great One. It was not sheer lunacy to hope for His coming.

Strange Happenings

But there were not only these ancient prophecies and current conditions to fan Jewish hopes of a *Messiah*, an "anointed deliverer" for the nation. There were, so the Gospels assure us, some very strange events that attended the birth of the boy in the stable.

First, His parentage. Matthew and Luke are the only two Gospels that record the birth and youth of Jesus, and they are both clear that although Joseph was the legal father of Jesus, he was not the biological father. We are told, in these two independent accounts, that Jesus was born by the direct action of God, the source of all life, in the womb of Mary, His mother, who was at that time still a virgin. This seems highly unlikely. Is the story made up, perhaps, to parallel pagan legends of virgin births? Or is it a misunderstanding of Isaiah 7:14 "a virgin shall conceive and bear a son," where, in the original language, *virgin* sometimes means merely a "young woman"?

The trouble is that the sober New Testament accounts of the annunciation to Mary, that she would have a child who would be known as God's Son, have nothing in common with the pre-Christian myths of intercourse between bearded gods and nubile young women. The gospel writers were better aware than we of the ambiguity of Isaiah's *virgin* and would be most unlikely to build a case on that one word—and get it wrong! And when we look more closely, we find that all the evidence suggests that there *was* something different about the birth of Jesus. Mark's gospel calls Him "the carpenter, the son of Mary" (6:3). The rabbis called Him "the bastard of a wedded wife" or "the son of an adulteress." The apostle Paul calls Him "born of a woman," and even the Koran calls Jesus *Isa ibn Mariam*, "Jesus the Son of Mary," and esteems Him as the virgin's Son, conceived by the creative word of God. Within a few decades of His death the birth of Jesus to a virgin had become one of the major points of Christian conviction and entered very early into the Creed. He was "born of the virgin Mary."

Now, of course, you can never prove a thing like that, to which there is no precedent and no sequel. But every shred of evidence we have points to the birth of Jesus as being different. Joseph had nothing to do with it. Was Mary unfaithful? That is how the opposition saw it. Or did God decide to intervene in this remarkable way when sending His Deliverer into the world? That is how the Christians came to see it. If Jesus really is both God and man, as the Christians became convinced, it would certainly be appropriate (though equally certainly not *necessary*) if Jesus was born of the virgin Mary and the creative *fiat* of almighty God.

The second remarkable thing that attended His birth was a very bright star over Bethlehem. Matthew's gospel tells us that astrologers (the Magi) had seen an unexpected star in the East and had come to worship the being it denoted. In the year 7 B.C. there was a conjunction between the planets Jupiter and Saturn three times in the portion of the sky known as "The Fishes," a phenomenon that happens only once in 794 years!

The stars all had a meaning to the men of antiquity. "Jupiter" denoted a world ruler, "Saturn" was considered the star of Palestine, and "The Fishes" indicated the last days. Plainly, therefore, this meant that the ultimate ruler of the world would appear in Palestine this year. We do not *think* people understood it in this way. We happen to *know* that they did. Cuneiform tablets (the ancient equivalent of newsprint) have turned up in Sippar in Babylonia (the Greenwich of the ancient world) written in 8 B.C. and foretelling this rare conjunction of Jupiter and Saturn the next year. That is why the wise men set out on their journey of discovery. That is why they turned up at Jerusalem, Palestine's capital city, looking for the world ruler that would spring from Judea.

This altered King Herod. Any such new pretender to power would be a threat to his own position. And so when he discovered that the wise men had gone to Bethlehem and had taken costly gifts to signify their obeisance to a baby boy born there, he ordered the massacre of all male children under two in that village. There could have been only a few dozen of them: it was not a big place. But it shows how seriously Herod took the threat posed by Jesus. Clearly this was no ordinary baby. Could He really be destined for world dominion? It was not worth taking any risks. Send in the soldiers.

Some have wondered why this event finds no record in secular history and if Herod would do such a thing. They are innocent folk! Herod was a very nasty piece of work. History shows that his reign was marked by a trail of executions without trial, and that he even had his own wife put to death. He had two of his sons strangled. He wrought carnage among the Pharisees and among his own courtiers. And as he lay dying he gave orders to have all the leading men of Jerusalem slaughtered at the hour of his death. To such a man, a deed like the execution of the Bethlehem infants was a very small episode.

The unusual birth; the star; the attendant massacre because the king feared he might be threatened — these are all remarkable accompaniments of the birth of Jesus. No wonder men wondered if this boy would prove the fulfillment of the nation's hopes. Were they right? We must read on and then make up our minds.

The Very Beginning

But first we must face the question with which this chapter began, "Where did it all start?" at yet a deeper level. John, the closest disciple of Jesus, chose to begin his gospel not in Bethlehem's stable but at the very beginning — in eternity. His claim is breathtaking:

> In the beginning was the Word, and the Word was with God, and the Word was God....All things were made through him, and without him was not anything made that was made. In him was life, and the life was the light of men (John 1:1, 3–4).

Who is he talking about? None other than Jesus. For he continues,

> And the Word became flesh and dwelt among us, full of grace and truth; we have beheld his glory, glory as of the only Son from the Father (John 1:14).

That is where the story starts, so John is convinced. The One who shares God's eternal being, the One who was His partner in the creation of the world, the One from whom light and life have their origin — this is the One we see in Jesus of Nazareth. John concludes that in all the previous ages of humankind "no one has ever seen God" but that now "the only Son who is in the bosom of the Father, he has made him known" (John 1:18).

That is where our story begins.

Or does it?

We must suspend judgment on John's staggering claim until we have taken a closer look at the life and teaching, the death and resurrection of this Jesus. Then we shall be in a position to make an informed decision about Him.

CHAPTER FOUR

~

What Did He Teach?

The first recorded words of Jesus run like this:

> Now after John was arrested, Jesus came into Galilee, preaching the gospel of God, and saying, "The time is fulfilled, and the kingdom of God is at hand; repent, and believe in the gospel" (Mark 1:14–15).

What an astonishing entry onto the scene by this thirty-year-old carpenter!

John the Baptist

His cousin John the Baptist had set the country alight with his teaching. He dressed and spoke like one of the ancient prophets of Israel. He told people that they had to stop playing with religion and repent, that is, change their whole attitude and behavior. God was going to lay the axe at the root of His tree, Israel, and dead wood would be hacked down and thrown into the fire. John was very specific. He assailed religious arrogance, social injustice, and personal apathy. This remarkable man was certain that he stood at the edge of the most crucial happenings in history. So he called people to prove their repentance by allowing him to baptize them in the muddy waters of the Jordan.

Nobody had ever done this to Jews before. It was a very radical step. Those who took it were admitting that being a member of the Jewish nation was not enough, that trying to lead a good life was not enough, and that regular attendance at the temple and the synagogue was not enough. They were looking for a complete cleansing through baptism from all that was bad in their lives. They wanted, in this symbolic action, to renounce all reliance on religious privilege, cast themselves on the mercy of God, and be prepared to meet the Messiah when He came. For John had made it very plain that his was only a preparatory ministry. He was preparing the way for God's Messiah.

The country was like dry tinder, and John supplied the spark. Nothing like it had been seen in Palestine for a century and more. He even dared to rebuke the ruler of Galilee, Herod Antipas, for his scandalous matrimonial affairs. This did not go down well. Antipas arrested John and threw him into prison. Ultimately he would have his head cut off. But in the meantime Jesus stepped out of the wings onto center stage. His message was a direct sequel to John's: the same call to repentance and radical change. But there was a fascinating new component: "The kingdom of God is at hand."

The Kingdom of God

The kingdom of God lies at the heart of what Jesus had to say, so it is important to grasp what it means.

As we have seen, many different groups in Palestine were looking for the kingdom of God. Of course, they interpreted it in many different ways. But they were all waiting for it—apart, perhaps, from the Sadducees, who were moderately content with the political and religious compromises that kept them in power. But everyone else was eagerly longing for the day when God would step in for His beleaguered people, defeat the hated Romans, and bring His rule to bear. So "the kingdom of God" was a phrase packed with power. And here was this carpenter claiming that with His arrival it was already at hand!

If you study the phrase "kingdom of God" in the Gospels, you will find that the primary meaning is God's sovereign rule. The trouble is that most people are rebels against God's way of doing things and want to paddle their own canoe. They are still within the realm of God's sovereign rule, of course, but are rebel subjects. And so the phrase "the kingdom of God" comes to have a secondary meaning: the people who willingly accept God's rule in their lives, seek to live by it and extend it.

Imagine, therefore, the excitement when Jesus followed John's call to radical change by this proclamation that the long-awaited kingdom of God was at hand. He was proclaiming it. He was bringing it in. No wonder the crowds materialized from nowhere and gathered around Him. Surely this would be the time for the decisive defeat of the Romans!

But Jesus had a great surprise for them. During His first address in His home synagogue in Nazareth He read the portion of Isaiah that says,

> The Spirit of the Lord is upon me, because he has anointed me to preach good news to the poor. He has sent me to proclaim release to the captives and recovering of sight to the blind, to set at liberty those who are oppressed, to proclaim the acceptable year of the Lord (Luke 4:18–19).

Then He added, to their amazement, "Today this scripture has been fulfilled in your hearing" (Luke 4:21).

No wonder the excitement was intense. Could it be that this young carpenter was the One who would bring deliverance to the chosen people from their hated Roman overlords? However, two rather ominous notes were struck. For one thing, Jesus said nothing about any military campaign, and He concentrated on the more spiritual aspects of the Old Testament hope. For another, He ended His quotation of Isaiah in a very significant place. Isaiah goes on to say "to proclaim...*the day of vengeance of our God.*" Jesus left that out. That is not what He has come for. And that would prove very disappointing to many people. For centuries the Jews had seen "the day of the Lord" as a future single event, bringing blessing to Israel and judgment to everyone else.

Jesus changed all that. He split "the day of the Lord" or "the kingdom of God" (they mean much the same) in two. Part of those ancient prophecies and that fervent expectation He had come to fulfill then and there: liberation. The other part, judgment, would have to wait until the end of history when, He told them, He would be back.

So what would it look like, this kingdom of God that Jesus had come to inaugurate? He describes it in His most famous address of all, the Sermon on the Mount. It is a prescription for the supremely happy life, lived as God intended. We shall see how radical it is if we contrast it with secular society's program for the happy life. J. B. Phillips has done it superbly:

Happy are the "pushers": for they get on in the world.
Happy are "the hard-boiled": for they never let life hurt them.
Happy are they who complain: for they get their own way in the end.
Happy are the blasé: for they never worry over their sins.
Happy are the slave drivers: for they get results.
Happy are the worldly wise: for they know their way around.
Happy are the trouble makers: for they make people take notice of them.

And then, with his marvelous gift of translation, J. B. Phillips presents the contrasting prescription that Jesus gives for the happy life, the life in the kingdom:

Happy are the humble minded, for they already belong to the kingdom of heaven.

Happy are those who know what sorrow means, for they will be given courage and comfort.

Happy are those who claim nothing, for the whole earth will belong to them.

Happy are those who are hungry and thirsty for goodness, for they will be fully satisfied.

Happy are the kindhearted, for they will have kindness shown to them.

Happy are the pure in heart, for they will see God.

Happy are those who make peace, for they will be known as sons of God.

That is what it looks like, life following the Maker's instructions. And Jesus goes on, in this marvelous sermon, to spell out what it means and what it takes.

It is a life of attractive goodness, quite different from the long-faced ethics of the religious. It will be like salt giving savor to a dish of food or a light giving direction to folk fumbling around in the dark. People in the kingdom will realize that the wish is father of the deed, and therefore that hatred is as obnoxious to God as murder, and lust as adultery. Divorce is not the way of the kingdom: God made the two to be — and remain — one flesh, and everything else is a fall from that ideal. The disciple is to be marked in several ways. His word will be his bond: no need for flowery oaths. Forgiveness will be his way of life, even when wronged. Love, even love for his enemies, will be the supreme mark of the follower of Jesus. You see, God is like that. And it begins to rub off.

Well, I can't describe it all. You must read it for yourself in Matthew's gospel, chapters 5 — 7. The disciple will live a life of generosity, of modesty, of prayer. He will not show off. He will not hoard his money but will give a lot of it away, tor his real investment is in heaven. He will be totally single-hearted, and his life will be marked by a marvelous peace. After all, God looks after the flowers and the grass and the birds. Can He not be trusted to look after us? What then is the point of worrying? Or of amassing great wealth or fine clothes? That is the way of secular society. But, Jesus said, "seek first his kingdom and his righteousness, and all these things shall be yours as well" (Matt. 6:33). But nobody drifts into this wonderful kingdom that Jesus came to usher in. You have to ask, to seek, to knock. You have to enter through a narrow gate. You have to build your very life on the rock of Jesus.

Amazing stuff, is it not? But that is a thumbnail sketch, from the lips of Jesus Himself, of what life in the kingdom is all about. No wonder people flocked around Him. They were tremendously attracted by His program. It had the ring of truth about it. And they were immensely drawn to His person; they had never seen a Man like Jesus.

But there was another side to this kingdom of God, and Jesus had a lot to say about it. It has a future as well as a present dimension. The day will come when all the hopes of the Old Testament prophets will be fulfilled. There will be a new heaven and a new earth, where peace and justice will rule. God's will shall in fact be done on earth as it is in heaven. The day will come when the dead will be judged and their final destiny determined. The day will come when God's kingdom comes to its complete fulfillment. But that day was not yet. However, His disciples must stay alert because they could never know when that last day of history would dawn, and He, the carpenter of Nazareth, would return in the glory of God to complete what He had begun when He was their companion and leader on earth. The kingdom of God had an "already" and a "not yet" aspect to it.

It's a wonderful thing, this kingdom of God. Jesus was insistent that we should not miss it at any price. It is no less than God's best plan for every human life.

The Fatherhood of God

If the kingdom of God was the major theme of the teaching of Jesus, the fatherhood of God runs it a very close second. What, I wonder, is your image of God? Someone who is noting down all your failures? Someone who does not want to see you happy? Someone who is tough and harsh and a bit mean? Someone who is too far removed to bother about you at all? Someone who is so holy that you have no hope of getting to Him anyway? Well, the contemporaries of Jesus shared some of those views. God was very important to them, but He was very far removed, too holy to approach except with the morning and the evening sacrifices offered daily in the temple at Jerusalem. He was the judge of all humankind — and His standard was perfection.

But Jesus brought an entirely new picture of God into the world. He was Father. You can search Islam, and you will not find that name of Father among the ninety-nine names of God. You will search Hinduism or Confucianism in vain. This is amazing good news, and it is unique. Jesus used the name *Abba* of His relationship with God. It means "Daddy." It was the intimate, family word that the Hebrew child used of his dad. Nowhere in all the history of Israel had it been used by anyone of God. That would have been unthinkable. Yet the carpenter from Nazareth confidently referred to God by this intimate, family name. He said that His relationship to God was like son to father. And the truly astounding thing was this: He told His followers that they could call God *Abba,* too.

The heart of the good news is wrapped up in that little Aramaic word, *Abba.* Failures like you and me, sinners like you and me, people estranged from God like you and me, can come into His very family and call Him Daddy. At the center of the kingdom of God is a loving Father. He extends His mercy to us who do not deserve it. He promises to adopt into His family those who are really a disgrace to it. He offers to put the family fortune in our hands and to employ us in the family business. Above all, He is willing for us, when we pray, to say, *"Abba,* who art in heaven . . ." He wants us, yes, He wants us, to know Him in this intimate way. Jesus did not come to proclaim a new set of religious duties or found a new religion. He came to show us that God is Father, and that there is nothing He wants more than to enfold us in His arms and welcome us home.

The Primacy of Love

At the heart of the kingdom is a Father. This leads on to the third staggering thing Jesus taught: the supremacy of unconditional love.

Judaism in the first century was dominated by three things: the temple at Jerusalem, with all its ritual sacrifices; the Sabbath day, around which an overwhelming burden of prohibitions had gathered; and the law of God, originally given to Moses on Mount Sinai and written down in the Old Testament but interpreted in minute detail by the clergy of the day. Temple, law, Sabbath — these three. If you wanted to please God, this was the threefold route you must tread. You must go to Jerusalem at the great festivals. You must keep the Sabbath holy and go to synagogue to learn from the religious leaders. And you must study the law of God and obey it meticulously. Do, do, do!

Jesus changed all that. He drove the money changers out of the temple and told the religious leaders that One greater than the temple was among them. He repeatedly healed people on the Sabbath day, so as to demonstrate that He was in charge of the Sabbath, not vice versa. And He gave His followers a new law — to love one another as He had loved them. Revolutionary stuff, and in the end it goaded the religious authorities to hound Him to death. He had set Himself up against the whole religious establishment!

But do you not see what He was saying? It is not religious ritual, however worthy, that brings you into the kingdom of God but a lovely filial relationship with Him. God does not want endless servants: He wants sons and daughters. It is not a question of doing lots of things for God: it is a question of allowing Him to become your loving heavenly Father and being true to that relationship. It will inevitably lead to a life of love to God and to your fellows. It is hardly surprising, in the light of all this, that the Christian word for "love," *agape*, was practically introduced into the language by Jesus. It did exist beforehand — just. But until He came, nobody had seen what it really meant. Yet, if God so *loved* the world that He gave His only Son for us, why, that shed an entirely new light on love. It meant total self-giving for the totally unworthy. That is what God the Father did. That is what Jesus embodied. That is what He called on His disciples to do.

The Call for Decision

I must not shrink from telling you the fourth great strand in the teaching of Jesus. He taught the vital importance of making a response here and now. The intriguing thing is that while He called people into the kingdom, He also called them to Himself. There is a fascinating part in Mark's gospel, chapter 10, where Jesus uses a number of specific words He tells *us* that if *we* want to be "saved," to "enter into the kingdom of God," to "have eternal life" there is just one condition: we must come, follow Him. Quietly but firmly He equated entering the kingdom of God with becoming His disciple.

He came into the world to inaugurate the kingdom of God. Those who wanted to enlist as members had to give their oath of allegiance, so to speak, to Him. This decision was very urgent. He proclaimed it passionately Himself. He sent His disciples into the towns and villages of Palestine to proclaim it. He gave fuller content to the repentance teaching of His predecessor John the Baptist. John had told people to turn from their sins in preparation for the coming deliverance. Jesus told them the Deliverer was here. They must have faith in Him, and entrust themselves to His little company. It may have seemed crazy, but it was essential. The new kingdom would grow and become effective only as rebel subjects rejoined their King.

That was the clarion call that went out throughout Palestine in the late twenties of the first century. It has been going out ever since. And it has brought some 1.5 billion people into the kingdom of God in our day alone, leaving aside all previous generations. It is very appealing but also very challenging. For Jesus made it crystal clear that our eternal destinies hang on our decision. He spoke more about heaven and hell than any other preacher there has ever been. He made it plain that you could be either safe with God or lost without Him. You could build either on the rock of Jesus and His teaching or on the sand of anything else — and that sand would prove no adequate foundation in time of flood. You could be a sheep in His flock, if you were willing, or you could remain a goat outside it. You could accept His invitation to the wedding feast, or you could stay outside in the dark. You must choose. Decision is urgent, says Jesus, and the time is now.

No wonder the ordinary people welcomed Him. No wonder the religious authorities were very dubious. They had too much to lose. And to ally themselves with Jesus, the local carpenter, was altogether too demeaning. But it was impossible in those days to evade the challenge of decision about Jesus. He compelled a decision. And still He does. You cannot sit on the fence. You have to decide. That is the unwelcome but realistic element in His teaching that none of us can evade. This disturbing Man faces us with a decision we would much rather not have to make. But relentlessly, yet lovingly, He says to us, "God's way of living, God's kingly rule, has come your way. I have brought it in person. Do you want to run your life that way, the best way? Or will you stay as you are and miss what you were made for? You must decide."

CHAPTER FIVE

~

What Did He Do?

"The kingdom of God does not consist in talk but in power" (1 Cor. 4:20) — those words of the apostle Paul are a reflection of the impact that Jesus had made on him. Unfortunately, some contemporary expressions of Christianity give the opposite impression. "The kingdom of God does not consist in power but in talk."

It would have been no good Jesus *talking* about the kingdom of God if He did not *do* anything about it. He did not come simply to proclaim the kingly rule of God but to bring it to bear directly on our everyday lives. In a word, He came to bring healing to a broken world. That is what *salvation* means: God's wholeness, His rescue at every level of our need. That is what Jesus set about doing, and He did it so effectively that enormous crowds constantly gathered around Him to share in the undreamed-of benefits He was bringing to ordinary people in need.

The Great Physician

Early in His ministry (as His two or three years of public, high-profile activity are often called), Jesus likened Himself to a doctor and remarked to some self-satisfied people who disapproved of the disreputable company He was keeping, "Those who are well have no need of a physician, but those who are sick; I came not to call the righteous, but sinners " (Mark 2:17).

When you stop to think of it, that is a very apt analogy. Jesus is so wholesome, so full of love and humor, of honesty and generosity, that beside Him we all show up as pallid and sickly. It is as if a husky athlete who had been bronzed by sun and surf, and was in superb shape from rigorous training, were to visit a hospital ward. What a contrast he would make to the unhealthy complexions, the bandaged limbs, the poor appetites, the malfunctioning bodies of the patients. It is only as they see this example of health that they realize how sickly they are. Just comparing themselves with one another, they might be quite pleased with the progress they had made or the strength they had partially regained. And when the doctor makes his rounds each day and asks how they are, they say, "I'm doing fine, thanks." Ah, but when the bronzed athlete comes in, they realize how sick they have been and what a long way they still have to go.

It is a bit like that when Jesus visits the human hospital we call our world. We think we are doing fine. We may think our ailments are not so disabling as those of others, our fractures are not so serious. But Jesus takes one look at us and, not in pride but in deep compassion, says, "You need a doctor. I have come to heal the sick."

And that is what you find Him doing for the great majority of all His recorded actions. He is reaching out with God's own compassion, which is the very lifeblood of the kingdom, to a sick society.

Dealing with Disease

You notice it most, as you read the Gospels, with His physical healings. There are an enormous number of physical healings attributed to Jesus. These were not occasional cherries on the cake of a task that was something different. *They were the cake!* Day after day you find Him healing people who were blind, lame, deaf. He restores mobility into limbs that had shriveled away. He even touches the untouchable, the lepers, and brings them back to health—an absolutely unheard-of thing. On two or three occasions He is even recorded as bringing back to life someone who had died. Now is all this just an act of compassion? No. It is that, of course, but it is far more. It is proof, for those with eyes to see, for those whose prejudices do not blind them, that the kingdom of God has broken in, that God's rule of wholeness has taken root.

Dealing with Demonic Forces

Jesus' healings were not confined to physical conditions. One of the most fascinating aspects of the gospel story is the tremendous outbreak of demonic activity during His lifetime. As so often happens, the presence of the best provoked the worst. The light of Jesus stimulated the darkness of evil.

The Bible is very clear that there is a devil, a supreme anti-God force, and I should have thought that the evidence is pretty impressive for his existence. Not, of course, a joke figure with cloven hoof and forked tail, but an organizing spirit behind all the wickedness, war, and disease among humankind—the ultimate opponent of God and goodness. Until the New Age erupted, with its channelers and spirit guides, until a new outbreak of satanism hit Western society, we scornful rationalists had been very skeptical of the reality of these evil spiritual forces. But we were a tiny, pampered minority. All down the centuries and all over the world people have recognized the reality of these malign powers and still do. And certainly in the Gospels there is no beating about the bush. Jesus believed in Satan. Jesus wrestled with him in the three spectacular temptations recorded in the Gospels and continued to fight him every step of the way to the cross itself. And those same Gospels are insistent that Satan has dark forces at his command that can and do affect human beings; the gospel writers call such people "demonized." It has been fashionable to laugh at such ideas, claiming that demonization is only a primitive explanation of what we now know as psychological illness. But that is a very ignorant view. Demonization is not the same as psychological illness at all.

This is not the place to go into the matter in any depth. I have tried to do so in *I Believe in Satan's Downfall*. It is enough here to notice three great differences. Demonization normally takes root in someone's life after the person has been involved in the occult; psychological illness does not. Demonization only shows itself spasmodically; psychological illness is generally operative all the time. And demonization, in contrast to psychological illness, responds to the command in the name of Jesus for the oppressive force to leave, and the person's restoration is immediate and lasting.

At all events, a major strand in the Gospels is that Jesus cast out these evil things from lives they were ruining. And I believe it, for I have seen the same thing happening time and again today. The expulsion of dark forces was then, and is now, a spectacular aspect of the coming of the kingdom of God. It is salutary to reflect that the Pentecostal church, which was born only in A.D. 1900, majors on this ministry of deliverance. It is hardly a coincidence that it is by far the fastest growing church in the world. Statistics suggest that more than one-third of all Christians in the world today have become touched afresh by the Spirit of God and are awakened to "spiritual gifts," which include the ability to set people free from the infestation of these evil powers. We must not exaggerate this aspect of Christianity. But neither must we minimize it. Jesus found the casting out of demons a significant part of His bringing healing and rescue to humankind. We should not be too surprised if the same thing happens today.

Dealing with Sins

But the wholeness or salvation that Jesus brought, as He came preaching the kingdom of God and exhibiting its power, did not stop at the physical and the demonic. By far the greatest healing Jesus wanted to effect was rescue from the ravages of sin.

There is such a thing as breaking God's laws. There is such a thing as failing to live up to His standards. There is such a thing as being a rebel against Him. All this brings guilt, real guilt — being in the wrong with God. And it matters. It is as lethal as a cancer, growing big and life-threatening inside a body that, for a while, feels there is nothing wrong. It was this hidden cancer, this being in the wrong with God, that Jesus was most anxious to reverse. His whole life was devoted to exposing this disease and putting it to rights. The final medicine would be distilled only at the cross of Calvary, and to that we shall turn in a later chapter. For the moment it is enough to notice the emphasis Jesus placed on this most serious of all diseases, and His passion to heal it.

On one occasion, a paralyzed man was brought to Him in the most difficult circumstances. The crowd around Him was so dense that the group bringing their friend to Jesus could not get through. So they hit on the brilliant idea of climbing the outside steps to the thin mud-and-wattle roof that was characteristic of the Palestinian house. They broke away some of the roofing and let their friend down on a mattress in front of Jesus. What did this pathetic, paralyzed specimen of humanity most need? It was obvious: he needed healing. But Jesus saw his need more profoundly. He said to him, "Your sins are forgiven" (Mark 2:5).

You can imagine what flutterings that caused in the ecclesiastical dovecotes! They thought it blasphemy. After all, who can forgive sins but God? Who indeed? And so Jesus says to them in effect, "It is all very well to say, 'Your sins are forgiven,' and nobody can tell whether they are or not. But if I say to this poor man, 'Get up and walk,' it will be perfectly obvious to everyone whether I speak from God or not. So in order to show you that the Son of man (His favorite name for Himself) really has power to do on earth what God does in heaven" — He broke off and said to the paralyzed man, "Get up, take your mattress, and go home." And he did! A perfectly staggering story. But don't miss the most shattering part of all. Jesus regarded the forgiving of this man's sins as much more important than the healing of his body.

Of course this man was not the only example of Jesus' going to the very root of human sickness and engaging with human sin. There are many others. One is the tax gatherer Zacchaeus, a nasty piece of work with whom Jesus invited Himself for a meal! And what a meal that must have been. Out of it Zacchaeus emerged a forgiven man, and he showed it by the way he offered to give back fourfold to anyone he had swindled, and in addition to give half of his estate to the poor. That man had lived for money: he had made everything subservient to amassing it. And then he saw it for what it was and was willing to let it go. Why? Jesus gives the answer: "Today salvation [or God's own total healing] has come to this house" (Luke 19:9). That is why.

Another example is a famous woman in the Gospels, Mary of Magdala, a little village on the northwest of the Sea of Galilee. We are told that she had been afflicted with no less than seven demons, and Jesus had set her free. She had been a prostitute, and Jesus had ministered to her God's forgiveness and given her back her self-respect. The result? She became a new person, full of love and loyalty to Jesus who had transformed her life. That is what forgiveness does. It makes new people of us. And that, above all else, is what Jesus came to do.

Jesus came to bring healing at every level: healing of body, healing from the malign influence of dark forces, healing from sin. The question of our chapter is, "What did He do?" The Gospels are unambiguous about the answer: He healed all manner of sickness and disease among the people (see Matt. 4:23).

Jesus and Miracles

But to say this lands us in a big problem, the problem of miracles. How can we in the twentieth century be expected to believe in miracles? Well, you simply cannot disentangle Jesus from miracles. Scholars in the last century tried very hard to discover a nonmiraculous Jesus. They utterly failed. Every single strand of material in the Gospels shows Jesus as Someone who was different in His powers from other people. Through Him God acted in a way impossible to understand if we think of Him simply as a good Man. The miracles begin at His birth, without human father. They continue in His ministry: miracles of healing and of exorcism, nature miracles (such as His feeding of the multitude or His walking on the sea in a storm), and supremely His raising from the dead Lazarus, the widow of Nain's son, and Jairus's daughter. Last of all comes the greatest of miracles, to which we shall turn later: His own resurrection from the grave — not just to a further *span* of life but to a new *quality* of life over which death has no power. That is the only Jesus for whom there is any shred of evidence — a remarkable Being exercising unheard-of powers.

Can We Believe Them?

It is fashionable to discredit miracles. Such things do not happen. But why not? The laws of nature do not forbid them. A "law of nature" is simply the name we give to a series of observed uniformities. This is the way things happen. But if a contrary instance is well attested, the scientist will widen his so-called law to embrace both the uniformities and the exception. In the case of Jesus there is a lot of strong contemporary evidence, from His friends and His opponents alike, that He was the exception to the rule. The disciples were clear about His miracles. The Jews could not deny them but attributed them to the devil. And there is a fascinating piece of supporting evidence that is not as well known as it should be. It is a fragment of the first Christian apologist, a man called Quadratus, who wrote in A.D. 124 to commend the truth of Christianity to the Roman emperor, Hadrian:

> But the works of our Saviour were always present (for they were genuine): namely those who were healed, those who rose from the dead. They were not only seen in the act of being healed or raised, but they remained always present. And not merely when the Saviour was on earth, but after his departure as well. They lived on for a considerable time, so much so that *some of them have survived to our own day.*

Isn't it fascinating that the only passage of Quadratus that has survived should bear testimony to the most improbable aspect of Jesus' life, His miracles? It shows how confidently the early Christians could count on the impact not only of what Jesus said but of what He did.

But there are traces of His miracles in Roman and Jewish sources as well. Justin Martyr, writing in his *Apology* about A.D.

150, can say with casual assurance, "That he performed these miracles you may easily satisfy yourself from the *Acts* of Pontius Pilate." It was the same with the Jews. In the Gospels they are unable to deny the reality of the miracles: they simply assign them to the power of Satan. In the Acts of the Apostles we find Jews attempting to use the name of Jesus as a potent spell in exorcism! Later on this continued so much that some of the rabbis had to forbid Jews to heal in the name of Jesus! For the open-minded person, willing to be convinced if he or she has sufficient evidence, the conclusion is compelling. Jesus was no mere preacher: He exhibited miraculous powers, and not once or twice but continually.

What Do They Mean?

Are we supposed to be impressed by a series of conjuring tricks? What do the miracles of Jesus mean? They seem to me to show us at least four things.

First of all, the miracles of Jesus reveal a God who cares. He cares so much about the condition of poor, broken humanity that He comes in person to be the doctor, the rescuer. And wherever He goes, He demonstrates that divine compassion. Often exhausted by His work, He never once is recorded as having sent anyone away unsatisfied. He cared; He gave; He healed.

Second, the miracles constitute a claim by Jesus as to who He really is. The nature miracles are a good example of this. The Old Testament is clear that it is *God* who multiplies food and feeds the hungry, but on two occasions Jesus Himself does this for thousands of people. Do you see the implicit claim? Think of Jesus walking on the water of the turbulent Sea of Galilee. Was that to show off? Not at all. It was to teach the terrified disciples a crucial lesson: that Jesus does what God does. In the Psalms we read that it is God who stills the raging of the sea; when the waves rise, He stills them. But what God does in the Old Testament Jesus does in the Gospels! The conclusion is evident. Jesus embodies God, brings Him into focus, as nobody else has ever done. The miracles are acted claims. They point to who Jesus really is.

What is more, the miracles are pictures of what Jesus offers to do in the human heart. His opening the eyes of a blind beggar, Bartimaeus, is a picture of the new vision He offers to us all. His healing of paralyzed people is a picture of the new power He makes available to those who put their lives in His hand. His turning of water into wine shows how He can change the ordinary drudgery of life into high-octane living. His feeding of the multitude shows how He longs to be the bread that satisfies the believer's heart. His raising of Lazarus from the grave points to His ultimate offer: to give new and eternal life to all who trust themselves to Him. That is one of the main reasons why Jesus worked miracles. He wanted to make concrete before the imaginations of His contemporaries (and their successors) the spiritual revolution He was longing to bring about in their lives.

Finally, one of the purposes of the miracles is to pose an inescapable challenge. After all, when you have seen someone raised from the dead in your presence, you have to make some decision about the One who did it. Is He a quack? Or is He real? Does He operate by witchcraft? Or by the power of God? None of the miracles constitutes knockdown proof. But they cause you furiously to think. You have to decide about Jesus. Is He, or is He not, what He claims? Does He, or does He not, bring in the kingdom of God, not just with talk but with power?

These miracles of Jesus cannot be set aside. They are in fact the key to what He did. Almost every major action of Jesus recorded in the Gospels involves miraculous powers. He was bringing in the kingdom of God. And it could not be hidden.

Accordingly, this activity of Jesus had a twofold effect. It reinforced His call to discipleship. People heard Him say, "Come, follow Me." They heard His teaching, watched His life, observed His power, and came and followed Him. But there were others, and among them many of the religious establishment, who could not bear to observe these acts of power. They were already persuaded that Jesus was very bad news. He was a threat to their position. He had had no training in the theological colleges they ran. He was not ordained. Everything He stood for was a challenge and a rebuke to them. And these acts of power simply confirmed what they had suspected anyway — that His power and authority, His teaching and character derived not from God, the God whom they worshiped so assiduously, but from His archenemy, the devil. That is the conclusion they came to.

I think that a miracle always has this effect. It is never knockdown proof of divine activity. It is a challenge. Should we assign it to God? Or should we explain it away? The choice is ours. But one thing is sure: what Jesus did faces us with an inescapable decision. We cannot sit forever on the fence. We have to make up our minds. Did this Man come to bring God to us, or is He a fraud or, worse, an instrument of evil?

CHAPTER SIX

~

What Did He Claim?

We are suspicious, and rightly suspicious, of people with big mouths who go around boasting of their heredity or achievements. Jesus did not do that. If He had, I, for one, would have found it very difficult to believe Him. On the other hand, just supposing for a moment that He really was God who had come to our rescue, how should we expect Him to let us into this most amazing of all mysteries? I guess there would need to be several pointers.

We should expect His life to be a model for everyone, everywhere, a matchless life untainted by the greed and lust and hatred that disfigure the rest of us. It was just that.

We should expect His teaching to be the most marvelous ever offered to humankind. It was just that.

We should expect a blazing love that made God seem the supreme reality and the ultimate joy. That is precisely what we find.

So the stage is set. The background is there. If Jesus makes statements about Himself and His mission, there is reason to take them seriously. What does He say?

In His personal life, Jesus' modesty and simplicity are striking. He possessed no home. When discussion broke out with the religious authorities about paying tax to Rome, He had to say to them, "Show Me a coin," presumably because He had none on His person. He was a wandering teacher after He left His carpentry business. He was a member of a large working-class family. He had no income, no formal education, no powerful backers. He invited people to come to Him because He was gentle and humble in heart and they would find rest for their souls. And it was all true.

But when occasion came to indicate the Source from which His authority and appeal derived, the story was very different. Three strands of evidence unite to reinforce the claim that this was no specially gifted teacher but *God Himself* among His people.

His Actions

First there were His actions. We have taken note of some of these in the last chapter. His miracles were all implicit claims. The healing, the restoring that God almighty loves to do, was being done through Jesus. This was anticipated in the prophecies of the Old Testament:

> "Behold, your God . . . will come and save you."
> Then the eyes of the blind shall be opened,
>   and the ears of the deaf unstopped;
> then shall the lame man leap like a hart,
>   and the tongue of the dumb sing for joy (Isa. 35:4–6).

Precisely those things happened during the ministry of Jesus. For God literally had come to save them — and that is what the very name *Jesus* means: "God to the rescue." Blind people were enabled to see again, dumb people to speak, deaf people to hear, crippled people to walk. It was all part of God's rescue.

When you look at it this way, you see into the very heart of the miracles of Jesus. They are not fairy tales or conjuring tricks. They are windows into who He really is. He is the One who opens eyes that are blind to their need. He is the One who opens ears that are deaf to His call. He is the One who gives new power to limbs crippled by constant failure. His miracles are pointers, clear pointers, to who He is: God in the midst.

But the miracles are not the only actions of His life that make this claim. There are two other outstanding actions of Jesus that laid direct claims to the prerogatives of God.

The first one we looked at earlier. Jesus responds in love to a paralyzed man let down on ropes through the roof by ingenious friends as He was teaching in a room packed full of people. He tells the man that his sins are forgiven. The bystanders do not miss the point. "Why does this man speak thus?" they ask. "It is blasphemy! Who can forgive sins but God alone?" (Mark 2:7). Who indeed? That is precisely the point Jesus is making. And He not only goes on to heal the man, as if to reinforce the claim, but tells them straight, "The Son of man has authority on earth to forgive sins" (Mark 2:10) — for He is the delegate of God in heaven and carries out His gracious purposes.

The second divine prerogative to which Jesus lays claim is accepting worship. Simon Peter and his partners had had a fruitless night's fishing. As they come in, Jesus calls out, "Let your nets down again, on the right side of the boat." I don't suppose they welcomed this advice from a nonfisherman. But they did it. The result? They landed an unbelievable catch of fish. And Peter impulsively, but with a flash of true insight, fell down at Jesus' feet and worshiped Him. Jesus accepted the worship as His due! No good man would have done that. There are examples of native people offering worship to both Peter and Paul in the Acts of the Apostles. Both men recoil in horror from such a thing. Not Jesus. It was right for Him to accept Peter's worship, and He knew it.

But an even more memorable occasion occurred after the

Resurrection. Jesus had appeared to the apostles (as His leading disciples were called) in the Upper Room where they were hiding. But Thomas was missing; we are left to guess why. And when they told him about the risen Christ, he did not believe a word of it. He said, "Unless I see in his hands the print of the nails, and place my finger in the mark of the nails, and place my hands in his side, I will not believe" (John 20:25). He had to eat his words. Jesus did appear and invited him to apply his test. I don't for a moment imagine he did. He fell at Jesus' feet and worshiped Him. "My Lord and my God!" he cried (John 20:28).

Jesus' response was calmly to accept the worship and say, "Have you believed because you have seen me? Blessed are those who have not seen and yet believe" (John 20:29). That would be mind-boggling in any culture. But in Judaism it has the added significance that they were all passionate monotheists. They would not offer any kind of worship to any man or statue: only to God alone. The implications of Jesus' accepting worship are obvious. He knew it was His due. Humble though He was, full of love and service to all, He nevertheless knew who He was and where He had come from. "He had come from God and was going to God," as the apostle John put it (John 13:3). And sometimes, just sometimes, He accepted the worship due to God alone. It was the prelude to the worldwide worship that would follow.

His Promises

The actions of Jesus, then, stake a clear claim as to who He was. But so do His promises. He made promises so staggering that they are crazy unless they are true.

He promised that heaven and earth would pass away but that His words would not. Well, they certainly haven't yet. The Bible, which contains them, has the greatest circulation of any book in the world.

He promised that He would give His followers eternal life, that they would never perish, and that nobody would be able to pluck them from His hand. The way the majority of Christians die underlines that promise. They sense His utter reliability as they cross the last river.

He promised that God so loved that world that He gave His only Son so that whosoever believed in Him would not perish but have eternal life. Hundreds of millions of people have tested that promise and found it to be true. He does give new life. And remember, "eternal life" in the teaching of Jesus is not something that begins when you are dead. It is something that can start here and now. And even death cannot quench it.

He promised that He would give His life as a ransom for many and that He would take personal responsibility for their offenses. He did, on the cross.

He promised that the Spirit of God, long restricted to special people, would be generally available as a free gift after His death. On the day of Pentecost that promise was fulfilled, and ever since millions upon millions of Christians have known it to be true. In receiving the Spirit they have received Jesus. Living in the Spirit's reality and power, they have been basking in the company of Jesus.

He promised that He was the Way to God, the Truth about God, and the very Life of God. Millions know it is true.

Jesus promised that if anyone thirsts, he could come to Him and drink. And not only would he be satisfied, but figuratively speaking, out of his inner being would flow rivers of sparkling water. It's true.

He promised that He was not just guessing in His teaching

about God. He knew what He was talking about because He came from God. "We speak of what we know, and bear witness to what we have seen," He said. "No one has ascended into heaven but he who descended from heaven, the Son of man" (John 3:11, 13). You could not have it clearer than that. Jesus knows. His information about God is firsthand.

He promised that He would judge the world at the end of history. It would be He who separated the sheep from the goats and directed them to their final destiny. And the criterion would be simple: What response had they made to what they knew of Him?

The Gospels are full of the promises of Jesus. We have done no more than glance at a few. But they prepare us for His most daring of all assertions: "I and the Father are one" (John 10:30), and again, "He who has seen me has seen the Father" (John 14:9).

The promises of Jesus are utterly unique. There is not even a partial parallel to them anywhere in the world's literature. Shall we believe them or not?

His Claims

The third strand in our inquiry is the specific claims that Jesus made. They are highly significant, both in what they assert and in what they do not.

Most Jews, as they thought about the good days ahead when God would bring in His kingdom, linked that time with the arrival of the Messiah. He would liberate the country and bring untold blessings to its inhabitants in a new golden age. More than 50 times in the Gospels, and 280 times in the rest of the New Testament, Jesus is referred to as the *Messiah* or *Christ* (the words are Hebrew and Greek for the same thing, "anointed one"). But Jesus never unambiguously claims the title for Himself. It was too nationalistic, too misleading. So although it appears in every strand of early Christianity as a title for Jesus, we cannot be sure that He used it for Himself, though He was certainly executed as a messianic pretender. No, He did not go around proclaiming Himself the Messiah. But He did make other claims.

Far and away the most popular self-designation of Jesus was "Son of man." It appears more than eighty times in the Gospels and always on the lips of Jesus Himself. It is used in three ways. On a couple of occasions it refers to the present work of Jesus and His claim to be both Lord of the Sabbath and the forgiver of sins. But the remainder of the references point either to the agony of the Son of man, where He takes upon Himself the role of Isaiah's suffering sinbearer, or to the glorious future of the Son of man, who will return to His world at the end of time in the Father's glory to bring all history to a close. To be sure, "Son of man" is a marvelous title because it could merely, in Aramaic, be another way of saying "I," as "one" can be used in English. But in some cases the claim is too explicit to be brushed aside like that. At His trial Jesus said, "You will see the Son of man seated at the right hand of Power, and coming on the clouds of heaven" (Matt. 26:64). No wonder the chief priest thought he had an open-and-shut case when he heard those words: "Why do we still need witnesses? You have now heard this blasphemy" (Matt. 26:65). Blasphemy indeed — unless it were true!

Another title He used from time to time was simply "the Son." He told a marvelous story against the religious leaders of Israel. God, He said, was like a man who planted a magnificent vineyard and let it out to tenants. But when he sent his messengers to get some of the fruit each year, they were beaten and sent away empty-handed by the wicked tenants. Last of all he sent his much-loved only son, saying, "They will reverence my son."

They did not. They took him and killed him. And judgment would inevitably fall upon them. (See Luke 20:9–18.) The Pharisees at once understood, just as we all understand, who the "son" is. It is claiming for Jesus a unique filial relationship with God, something unheard of in Israel.

If you think of these two words, *Son* and *Father*, they are a brilliant choice. Jesus was a human being, not God in disguise. But He was not only a human being: He shared God's nature. What better imagery than Father and Son? A son shares his father's nature, and yet has his own distinctness. And the intimacy between father and son can be the greatest in the world. Jesus claimed that shared nature, that shared intimacy with almighty God.

Jesus' awareness of who He was comes out allusively in so many ways, particularly when He unself-consciously claims for Himself things that are attributed to God in the Old Testament. Let me show you what I mean.

In the Old Testament God alone is the Redeemer. "He will redeem Israel from all his iniquities," we read in Psalm 130:8. But Jesus comes along and says that He is going to give His life as a ransom for many! In the Old Testament "glory" belongs to God alone. "I am God. I shall not give my glory to another," we read (see Isa. 48). But what does Jesus say in the famous prayer recorded in John 17? "And now, Father, glorify me with the glory which I had with you before the world was made." Again, in the Old Testament it is the word of God that endures forever, in contrast to the flowers that fade. Jesus clearly accepted this high view of the revelation of God in the Old Testament. He said, "Till heaven and earth pass away, not an iota, not a dot, will pass from the law" (Matt. 5:18). Nevertheless He made precisely the same claim for His own words: "Heaven and earth will pass away, but my words will not pass away" (Matt. 24:35). His words are words of God; they last forever. Perhaps the most impressive of all is the Old Testament insistence that God alone is "Savior" and "Judge." But Jesus says He has come to seek and to save the lost on the one hand; and on the other, that the Father has committed all judgment into His hands.

It is in artless coincidences like these that I see the claims of Jesus seeping out so clearly. But there is one more explicit claim to which I would like to draw your attention. It is very significant, but it is not often noticed. It comes in two little words, *Ani hu* in Hebrew and *Ego eimi* in Greek, translated "I am." The force of these little words is often blunted in English translations because you can't just say "I am": you need to say "I am he" or something of the sort. But "I am" is the most holy name of God Himself in the Old Testament. He is the source of all life, the ever-living One. When Moses saw the bush burning without being destroyed in the deserts of Sinai, sensed God's presence, and dared to ask His name, the answer was "I am" — *Ani hu*. That name for God was not only much revered in Israel, it was much used and formed part of the liturgy of the Feast of Tabernacles and of Passover, where readings full of the "I am" were used such as the following:

> "You are my witnesses," says the LORD,
>   "and my servant whom I have chosen,
> that you may know and believe me
>   and understand that *I am* He.
> Before me no god was formed,
>   nor shall there be any after me.
> I, *I am* the LORD,
>   and besides me there is no savior....
> *I am* God, and also henceforth *I am* He;

~ 58 ~

there is none who can deliver from my hand;
I work, and who can hinder it?" (Isa. 43:10–13).

Well, that is exactly the claim we find Jesus making — the divine "I am." It is sometimes very explicit. Sometimes it is ambiguous. We are, as ever, left with the responsibility of assessing the evidence and making up our own minds.

We find it in Jesus' conversation with the woman of Samaria (see John 4). She wonders if Jesus could be the Messiah. He seems to correct her and says, "*I am*, I the one who is speaking to you." He could, of course, be agreeing with her suggestion that He is the Messiah; but remember, that is a title He did not use. So He may be making a much more radical claim: He is not the Messiah, as she thinks, but the divine "I am."

That is much more clearly the sense in the second instance. There is a freak storm on the Sea of Galilee. The disciples, hardened fishermen, are terrified. They are even more terrified when they see Jesus walking on the waves. He says to them, "Take heart. *I am*. Have no fear" (see Matt. 14:22–33). The divine name accompanies the divine action of stilling the storm.

Then, in debate with the Jews about Abraham, Jesus claimed that Abraham rejoiced to see His day. The indignant reply of His assailants was, "You are not yet fifty years old, and have you seen Abraham?" Jesus said to them, "Truly, truly, I say to you, before Abraham was, *I am*" (John 8:57–58). We are told that they picked up rocks to hurl at Him. They knew quite well what He was claiming.

Again, at the height of His trial, when the chief priest charged Him with being the Messiah, Jesus replied with those two same little words, *I am*. Did He mean He was the Messiah, something He had never claimed in His life? It could be so. But it is much more probable that He was using those words with all the depth of the Old Testament name of God behind them. Not just the Messiah but God in person. No wonder the chief priest tore his clothes and cried blasphemy!

And finally, on that precious last evening He spent with His disciples, He foretold the way Judas would betray Him and said, "I tell you this now, before it takes place, that when it does take place you may believe that *I am* he" (John 13:19). He wants, above all, for His followers to be sure of His identity.

There are mystery and ambiguity in these words, of course. Sometimes they may simply register agreement with what someone has asked. But that could never be said of so strange a claim as, "Before Abraham was, I am." We may be certain, I think, that Jesus did sometimes use this term with intent, to drive His hearers back to the sacred name of God in the Old Testament, a name that was being extensively studied in contemporary Judaism. The rabbis did not fail to take the point. Listen to one of them, Rabbi Eliezer, about A.D. 160:

> God saw that a man, son of a woman, was to come forward in the future, who would attempt to make himself God and to lead the whole world astray. And if he says he is God he is a liar. And he will lead men astray, and say that he will depart and will return at the end of days.

Listen to another, Rabbi Abbahu of Caesarea. He writes about a hundred years later but is quoting from a very early source:

> If a man says "I am God," he is a liar; "I am the Son of man" his end will be such that he will regret it; "I shall ascend into heaven," will it not be that he spoke and will not perform it?

These attacks are clearly directed against the remembered claims of Jesus. It is plain not only from the Gospels but from His enemies that Jesus claimed the right to the sacred name of God. It is Jesus' clearest and boldest statement about Himself. It has none of the pictorial language necessarily involved in concepts like "Son of man" or "Son of God." It is simple, direct, devastatingly bold. Jesus takes the name of God and claims it as His right. That is why He could be so sure that the kingdom of God was in their midst — for *He had brought it in!* When Jesus says, "I am," He means, "Where I am, there is God. Where I teach, there God teaches. Where I act, God acts. Where I promise, God promises. Where I suffer and die, God suffers and dies." It is impossible to imagine any claim more challenging. You can only say yes in adoring worship or no in fierce rejection of such a claim.

And what about you? The threefold evidence of His actions, His promises, and His claims sets Jesus apart from other men. Who do you say that He is? It is the most important judgment you will ever make. He confronts you head-on and says, "Make up your mind. Decide."

C. S. Lewis was a brilliant Oxford professor who found himself driven to make a decision on this issue. It profoundly altered his own life and, through his writings, the lives of millions of others. He reminds us that there is no halfway house over this issue. There is no parallel in other religions. Jesus is utterly unique. Lewis writes,

> The things he says are very different from what any other teacher has said. Others say, "This is the truth about the universe. This is the way you ought to go." But he says, "I am the Way and the Truth and the Life." He says, "No man can reach absolute certainty except through me. Try to retain your own life and you will inevitably be ruined. Give yourself away and you will be saved." He says, "If you are ashamed of me, if, when you hear my

call, you turn the other way, I will look the other way when I come again as God without disguise. If anything whatever is keeping you from God and from me, whatever it is, throw it away. If it is your eye, pull it out. If it is your hand, cut it off. If you put yourself first you will be last. Come to me, everyone who is carrying a heavy load, and I will set that right. Your sins, all of them, are wiped out. I can do that. I am Re-birth, I am Life. Eat me, drink me: I am your food. And finally, do not be afraid; I have overcome the whole universe." That is the issue.

It is indeed the issue. You have seen what Jesus claims. What do you say?

CHAPTER SEVEN

~

Why Did He Die?

In the spring of A.D. 30 the most ghastly miscarriage of justice took place. The leaders of the Jewish nation, the most God-fearing in all the world, handed over a young Man to the occupying forces to be tortured to death. He had done nothing wrong. The occupying power, with a worldwide reputation for justice, strung Him up on a rough wooden cross to die when the governor himself had three times declared Him innocent. Why?

His Death Was Inevitable

His death was inevitable for two reasons. First, because there is something very ugly and twisted in our human nature. We do not like seeing people who are better, kinder, and more unselfish than ourselves. We feel put in the shade by them. But imagine what it must have been like to have the moral perfection of Jesus of Nazareth moving around in your midst. It must have driven you wild. Wild, either with love and loyalty to Him or with hatred against Him and the determination that He must go. It is not so hard to understand the cry of the mob, "Crucify Him! Crucify Him!" It is not so hard to understand their preference for the imprisoned murderer and guerrilla leader, Barabbas. They could understand Barabbas. They could empathize with him. But Jesus . . . His goodness was uncanny. It was a threat. It must be removed if they were to have any peace. Some time previously Jesus had put His finger on this dark side of human nature. Our condemnation, He said, lies in this, that "light has come into the world, and men loved darkness rather than light, because their deeds were evil. For every one who does evil hates the light, and does not come to the light, lest his deeds should be exposed" (John 3:19–20). That is why His death was inevitable, given the quality of life He lived.

Second, Jesus had come into irreversible collision with the rulers of His nation. For one thing, the enormous popularity of His mission was rocking the stability of the fragile peace with Rome and was likely to bring down savage reprisals that would embroil the whole nation. But for another, Jesus seems to have set Himself against the whole fabric of Jewish religion, Jew though He was Himself. As we saw in an earlier chapter, the focal points of Jewish worship were the temple, with its sacrifices; the law, with its scribal exponents and its synagogue teaching; the Sabbath with its restrictions; and perhaps we might add circumcision, the seal of belonging for all Jewish males. But here was Jesus putting a massive question mark at the heart of all these prized indicators of Jewish separateness.

He told people that His person could be regarded as a timeless "temple" that God would raise up after His death and make the center of spiritual worship: mysterious words, which were not understood until later, but dangerous words, which were raised at His trial. They could be construed as blasphemy or magic, and both were capital offenses.

Then there was His attitude to the law. It was very embarrassing. On the one hand He seemed more at home in it than any of them, but on the other He was totally opposed to their literalistic interpretations of it, and was ruthless in His attacks on clerical dishonesty and hypocrisy.

He was apparently casual about the Sabbath regulations, too.

Why, He would go for a Sabbath walk in the fields and pluck some grain with His hands, rub it, and eat it: perfectly acceptable behavior in Israel but not on Saturday, the Jewish Sabbath! It was construed as reaping, threshing, and making a meal—a triple breaking of the clergy's "fence" around the Sabbath. Worse still, Jesus seemed to take delight in doing His cures on the Sabbath day, insisting it was a day to save life not to oppress it.

Nor did Jesus show the proper sense of propriety one would expect from a pious Jew toward the company He kept. He was often surrounded by the dregs of society, people with whom the pious would never dream of associating. It was His way of showing that God cared for bad characters as well as the respectable, but the Jewish clergy was scandalized. Worse, He was known to have defiled Himself by helping non-Jews: Romans, Syro-Phoenicians, and Samaritans—the uncircumcised scum. God loved them, too, of course, and Jesus was showing just that. But then, the Jewish clergy could not be expected to see it that way.

It is hardly surprising, then, that as early as the third chapter of Mark's gospel we find an unthinkable coalition of political irreconcilables among Israel's leadership deciding that Jesus had to go. As His ministry progressed, that conviction merely hardened. It was inevitable.

His Death Was Voluntary

But that is only part of the story. The death of Jesus was not merely inevitable. It was voluntary. That is the astonishing thing about it. He told His friends that nobody was taking His life from Him: He was laying it down of His own free will. He steadfastly set His face to go to Jerusalem, we read, when He knew quite well that by so doing He would be signing His death warrant. Three times, in that long journey up to Jerusalem, He told His friends that He was going to His death. And in the best-known description of Himself, as the Good Shepherd, He pointed out that the good shepherd is the one who is prepared to lay down his life for the sheep.

When He was arrested on that dark night in the Garden of Gethsemane, He could have asked His followers to fight. Instead, He told the only one who was armed to put away his sword and then, so the Gospels tell us, healed the man among His attackers whom that sword had injured. At His trial, when He could have spoken in His own defense, He preferred to stay silent. When confronted by the Roman governor who boasted of his powers of capital punishment or release, Jesus quietly told the governor that he could have no power whatsoever over Him unless it was allowed by God. Even as He hung on that terrible cross, He could have called on His heavenly Father to set Him loose, confident that He would have received immediate and decisive divine aid. But He did not cry to be set free. He determined to go through with it, although every nerve in His body shrieked its protest. There was something inexplicably voluntary about the death of Jesus, which sets it apart from all other horrendous deaths.

His Death Was Foretold

But even that recognition leads us only to the edge of the mystery of His death. For it was not only voluntary: it was predicted. As Jesus studied the Old Testament Scriptures He saw a thin red line of sacrificial death wherever He looked. It was there in the death of a lamb for each household that was instrumental in the Jews coming out of captivity in Egypt, the sacrifice that welded them into a nation. It was there in the sacrificial system that saw the death of animals on the altar morning and evening every day. It was there on the Great Day of Atonement when the high priest went into God's holy presence equipped with the blood of a sacrificial animal. It was there in every covenant that had ever been struck in Israel between the people and its God—except one. The new covenant that the prophets had talked about contained no mention of blood.

But Jesus could not help wondering if that apparent omission would soon be rectified. He knew how opposition and death had been the fate of the prophets. He knew that the son of man in Daniel's strange book was assailed by wild beasts. He knew that the awesome destiny of the Suffering Servant of God in Isaiah's prophecy had never yet been fulfilled. He knew that this majestic figure would have His right to justice taken away by oppression, that He could be cut off from the land of the living, stricken for a nation's sin. He knew that God's Suffering Servant would make His grave with the wicked and with a rich man in His death, although He had done no violence and there was no deceit in His life. This was all predicted by the prophet Isaiah. And yet out of this terrible fate and gruesome disaster God's purposes for good would prosper. He would see the fruit of His ordeal and know it was all worthwhile. He would make it possible for many, many to be put right with God because He would bear away their iniquities. This superb passage of Isaiah 53 ends like this:

> Therefore I will divide him a portion with the great,
>   and he shall divide the spoil with the strong;
> because he poured out his soul to death,
>   and was numbered with the transgressors;
> yet he bore the sin of many,
>   and made intercession for the transgressors.

Jesus knew all this. It was in His Bible. He sensed it applied to Him. And that is why He was convinced that

the Son of man will be delivered into the hands of men, and they will kill him; and when he is killed, after three days he will rise (Mark 9:31).

But the disciples, we read, did not understand His repeated warnings on this most unwelcome subject and were afraid to ask Him. Somehow Jesus was convinced His death, voluntary though it was, would prove to be the fulfillment of many hints, many prophetic utterances centuries old. "It is written," He said. It *must* be.

His Death Was Vicarious

But why was it written? And why did it have to be? We are getting near the heart of the cross of Jesus now. For that death was unlike all other deaths because of the One who suffered there.

All we have seen in this book so far goes to show that Jesus was not just a good man or a wonderful teacher. He embodied all of God that can become a human being: that is what the "Son of God" language of the New Testament means. Theologians talk about the two natures of Jesus; by that they mean He was both one with God and one with us: both divine and human. That is a simply staggering claim, but we have seen reason to suppose that no other explanation of who Jesus is will do. And if that is so, it sheds almost unbearably bright light upon the cross on which this marvelous person died.

First, His death on the cross was *an example of supreme love*. As we have seen He went there voluntarily. He went there for us. He was the Good Shepherd who laid down His life for the sheep. On one occasion He had said those immortal words:

> Greater love has no man than this, that a man lay down his life for his friends (John 15:13).

Actually, He displayed even greater love than this. For He laid down His life for the apathetic, for the hostile, for those who most certainly were not His friends. The apostle Paul can't get over the wonder of such love:

> Christ died for the ungodly. Why, one will hardly die for a righteous man—though perhaps for a good man one will dare even to die. But God shows his love for us in that while we were still sinners Christ died for us (Rom. 5:6–8).

What love that shows! What divine generosity to us human beings, who must seem so antlike from His perspective. He loved so much that He came among us. He loved so much that He taught us the way back to Him. He loved so much that He showed it in countless acts of kindness, healing, and power for the lonely, the diseased, and the oppressed. He loved so much that He put up with opposition that was totally unmerited. He loved so much that He was willing to face an unjust trial, the desertion of all His friends, the apparent failure of His whole life's work. He loved so much that He was willing to identify with His creatures in the worst agonies of suffering and death so that nobody would ever be able to point the finger at God and say, "He doesn't understand." He does understand. He has stood in our shoes. He has suffered as no one has ever suffered. He died the worst death it was possible to die. The Cross was an example of supreme love.

Second, the Cross was *a rescue from mortal danger.* This is something we willfully ignore. It is too embarrassing. We love to play Jesus off against other faiths or say, "Well, I can get to God my own way." The Cross puts a full stop to such folly. It tells us that we cannot get to God our own way. How can a bunch of rebels waltz back into the divine presence singing, "I did it my way"? The human race is in dire peril. Not only from international, social, economic, and ecological disasters. But from one more fundamental. We are out of touch with God, and most of us want to keep it that way.

He is a threat to our independence, a check on our pleasures and, worst of all, a judge of our actions. And so we distance ourselves from Him. Of course we do. It is only natural. And when God sees the alienation we have chosen instead of closeness to Him, He cannot remain indifferent. We are in the wrong, and He cannot pretend otherwise. And so the gap widens. And we who are so alive physically and mentally are spiritual corpses.

We are out of touch with God, so out of touch that we do not even realize the extent of our separation. All we realize is that sense of deadness, of alienation, of profound loneliness, of lack of meaning, of the inability of possessions to satisfy us who have made possessions our god. We have wandered deep into the wasteland, and we are perishing there. We have contracted an immense load of debts before God, and we have nothing we can pay. We have fallen prey to forces we cannot fight that hold us in captivity, and we desperately need someone to ransom us and set us free.

That is exactly where the cross of Jesus fits in. He did not die on that cross merely as an example, wonderful though that would have been. He died there to bridge that gap between us and God, to kill that hostility, to bring reconciliation instead of alienation.

He was the fulfillment of that Old Testament scapegoat who went out into the burning wilderness bearing away the sins of the nation. He was the ultimate Day of Atonement sacrifice through whom we could get right with the God we had so neglected and abused. He burdened Himself with the debts we could not pay, and before He gasped out His life in death He was able triumphantly to cry, "Finished." The debts were squared. The job was done.

And as for those forces that hold us in captivity, the evil habits, the false beliefs, the occult practices, and all the other foul things that spoil our world—all of them agents of the prince of darkness—well, on the cross "he disarmed the principalities and powers and made a public example of them, triumphing over them in him" (Col. 2:15). The Gospels have shown us that the real enemy was not, as the Jews thought, the Romans and their occupation of the Holy Land. The real enemy was the prince of darkness, Satan, the devil—call him what you will. It is he who lies behind all that is evil in this world. And it is with him that Jesus was determined to contend.

We see that struggle taking place in the temptations of Jesus at the outset of His ministry. We see it in the battles with the scribes and Pharisees. We see it in the prodigious amount of illness and demon possession Jesus encountered. It was all part of the relentless war. But the final showdown was the Cross. The temptation to avoid it was so great. And even once it was accepted, the ultimate assault of evil was so powerful, the weight of human sin so great, that He might still have failed. But He did not fail. He endured our doom. He shared our pain and mortality. He overcame our enemy. Had He not done so we would have had no chance whatever of entering the kingdom of God and being welcomed back into the family. Guilty, lost, and helpless, what could we have done to put ourselves in the right with God? Nothing at all. And that is why God went to such extreme measures in order to rescue us. That is why Jesus called His death "a ransom for many" (Matt. 20:28). And that is why the most sublime verse in all the Scriptures has such a realistic backdrop of mortal danger to it:

> For God so loved the world that he gave his only Son, that whoever believes in him
> *should not perish*
> but have eternal life (John 3:16, emphasis added).

Third, not only was the cross of Jesus a rescue from mortal danger for every one of us; it was also *a solution of complete fairness.* God had a problem with us. It stretched back to the first man. From the dawn of time we humans have chosen to go our own way. We have been rebels, hostile, ungrateful, and self-centered, experiencing all the human misery to which that self-centeredness leads. This is true, and we all know it. It is futile to deny it. The heart of our problems is the problem of our hearts. And what is God to do about it? He could, I suppose, force us to go His way, like a train, fated to follow the rails. But where, then, would be the free will with which alone we could respond to His love? He could, I suppose, condemn us to the permanent separation from Him that our lives deserve and that we have already chosen for ourselves. In that case there would be no hope for us. Or He could, perhaps, pretend that our sins and wicked deeds do not matter, pat us on the head, and imagine all in the garden is lovely when He knows — and we know — it is not. But God is not into a game of make-believe. Where would be His integrity, His justice, if He did that? Where would be the difference between right and wrong? No, none of these possible solutions had any mileage in it.

But in the cross of Jesus I see a solution of complete fairness: God could be totally just and fair, on the one hand, and could have people like us back into His company, on the other. What He did is breathtaking in its boldness, unassailable in its justice, and earthshaking in its generosity. He took our place! He condemned the wickedness of human beings and took the condemnation in His own person. He faced up to the poison in human hearts and drank the bitter cup of death Himself. He did not pretend that our debts to Him were not astronomical. But He paid for them out of His own account, and it crushed Him. Is that not the most incredible love?

Some people present it as a cold transaction, as if God the Father punished Jesus in our place. Often they back it up with legal analogies, which are less than just and less than helpful — as if a judge would cause (or even allow) the wrong person to be punished. That is not God's way. What He did was absolutely just and fair. It was the solution that gave complete satisfaction both to His holiness and to His love. He upheld the penalty we deserved — and then went and endured it Himself. And because Jesus was *human*, it was a person standing for the human race at the place of our greatest need. Because Jesus was *God* as well as man, the effect of what He has done is limitless. It explains how God could accept people like Abraham and David in Old Testament days who knew nothing of Christ but were clearly reveling in divine forgiveness. They were forgiven because of what Jesus was going to do on the cross. It explains how God can accept us, so many centuries later, because of what Jesus did, once and for all, on the cross. It explains how God may well be able to welcome people who genuinely seek Him but have no knowledge of Him because of their historical or religious circumstances. As John, that close friend of Jesus, put it:

[Jesus] is the expiation for our sins, and not for ours only but also for the sins of the whole world (1 John 2:2).

Finally, the Cross is a *pledge of total acceptance.* If I am honest about the failures in my own life, the evil I still do, the depths of wickedness to which I know I can and sometimes do still stoop, how can I be sure that God will still bother about me? After all, why should He? The answer lies in the cross of Jesus. Because He died there in actual and public agony, I know God will not go back on His contract with me, however much I mess up my end of it. The death of Jesus is the seal on the whole transaction. It is the marriage ring on the whole relationship. It is the adoption certificate into the family, the naturalization papers into the kingdom.

Whatever imagery you find helpful — this is the seal, this is the guarantee. So much that in John Bunyan's great classic *Pilgrim's Progress,* Christian's heavy burden fell off at the cross of Jesus and was seen no more, and he went on his way with freedom and joy. So much that the apostle Paul could exult, "There is therefore now no condemnation for those who are in Christ Jesus" (Rom. 8:1). None. My accusing guilt has been dealt with once and for all by what Jesus did for me on the cross. My acceptance in the family is assured not because of what I have done but because of what He has done. I shall never be thrown out for misconduct not because I deserve my membership but because He has guaranteed it. The warranty is written in His blood. Could any pledge be more trustworthy?

Sometimes when we encounter sheer generosity on a massive scale, we feel embarrassed. But at other times our eyes light up with wonder, and we throw ourselves into the arms of our generous benefactor. This is what Jesus Christ wants us to do in response to His breathtaking gift. The hymn writer put it well:

> Nothing in my hand I bring
> Simply to the cross I cling.

That is the only proper response to such a gift.

CHAPTER EIGHT

~

Was Death the End?

Did you wonder why this book is called *Who Is This Jesus?* rather than *Who Was This Jesus?* The answer is that Jesus is alive!

A Contemporary Experience

I sat next to the man on the old blue couch in my study in Oxford. I wept as I heard him blurt out a confession to God and simply ask the risen Christ to come into his life. And then the joy broke out. And the laughter. It was wonderful. It would have been wonderful if it happened once. But it has happened literally millions of times. You see, Jesus is alive, and once you put your life in His hands you discover the truth of it for yourself.

A group of us gathered around the young man's bed. He had a severe back injury. He had been lying there for weeks. And he was a Christian. As he read his New Testament he became convinced that God was calling him to invite responsible Christians, myself included (as pastor of his church), to pray for his recovery. As we prayed, I felt a deep assurance that God was healing him. So I told him to get up and walk around the courtyard. He did. Twice. I asked him to rest, and I went back home to get him a meal. We were all filled with joy at what God had done. This took place in Oxford University. That man is now a missionary in Africa. The living Jesus had healed him.

I watched another at worship last night. He is an enormously strong man who has lived for surfing in the big league and been a world champion. He loves it. But he loves Jesus a lot more. It stood out on his face, in his gestures, in his love last night as he worshiped and led a simple Communion service. He was in the midst of a congregation he had founded from among the tough young daredevil surfers of Hawaii. It was a moving occasion, for this was his last service before going to a new ministry on the mainland of the United States. This man, a businessman who had been captured by Jesus Christ, was worshiping not a dead cult figure last night but a living person. It was perfectly obvious from his radiant face, his words, his manner. Jesus was the person who had changed his life.

He had started a little Bible study among the surfers eight years ago because he could not keep quiet about this Jesus who had come to mean so much to him. Now he found himself a pastor of some hundreds of people. And they were all lighted up with this same discovery. Jesus is alive! They had sent missionaries out from their tiny Hawaiian island into Latin America and the Philippines. They had taken scores of their congregation for short-term outreach to foreign countries and had seen literally hundreds come to that same discovery that lighted them up: Jesus is alive!

I think of a woman I knew first when she was a prostitute, deep into witchcraft. It was a long and bitter struggle to see that woman set free. But I wish you could see her now. She is radiant in the friendship of a Jesus who is no dead figure of history but a living friend who has transformed her life. And she has declared as much in the very newspapers in which she had once cursed His name.

I have deliberately begun with experience. Because that is what it is all about, this Christian life. Real Christianity is not some coolly argued case, culminating in conclusions that are at best probable. It is a friendship with the risen Jesus. It is knowing this vibrant, living person for yourself. It turns your whole life sunny side up.

"Michael," I can almost hear you say, "you are just an enthusiast. You can't expect us to believe all that rubbish about a dead man coming to life again. This is the twentieth century!"

Yes, I agree. I am an enthusiast. But not just an enthusiast. There is strong evidence behind the enthusiasm. But I have not begun with the evidence. You see, people are seldom *argued* into the Christian faith. They *fall in love* with the risen Jesus once they meet Him. That is where it all begins.

But is this credible? Can we seriously suggest that Jesus of Nazareth left the tomb in which He was buried three days after His execution and is alive today?

Take a good hard look at the evidence. It will bear your scrutiny.

A Dead Body

First, the Man was dead. Jesus of Nazareth died in a horrible and very public manner on a Roman cross. Thousands witnessed it. He died in a comparatively short time: six hours. Was He really dead when He was taken down from the cross on that first Good Friday and laid in Joseph of Arimathea's tomb? Maybe He was still just alive? Maybe He revived in the cool of the tomb? Maybe that is how the Easter story began?

No, that won't do. He was dead all right. The Jews were very fussy not to have their Sabbath days defiled by bodies hanging on crosses. So it was politic for the Romans to take them down if they were well and truly dead. What they did was to take a big hammer and break the legs of the poor wretches who tried to gasp an extra breath or two by hoisting themselves up on their crosses by their legs. Crucifixion imposed the most terrible strain on the chest. Once their legs were broken they soon expired. But when they came to Jesus, the soldiers found He was dead already. So they did not break His legs. One of them simply stuck his spear into the side of Jesus and pierced His heart. Had Jesus still been alive, bright arterial blood would have come out of the wound. As it was, an eyewitness, probably His friend John himself, tells us that out of that wound came blood and water. This is a totally prescientific description of what the mixture of dark blood and translucent serum would have looked like. And the separation of blood from serum is one of the strongest legal and medical proofs of death. He was dead all right. The executioner certified His death to Pilate, the governor of the province. If he had gotten it wrong, his own life would have been on the line. If Pilate got it wrong, his job would have been on the line. Neither of them got it wrong. The Man was dead. The body was given to a couple of His followers for burial. So we can rule out of court any of those theories about Jesus reviving in the cool of the tomb. There was no reviving. He was dead.

An Empty Tomb

The next thing to notice is that the tomb of Jesus was empty on the first Easter Day. That is the Christian claim, and nobody was able to deny it. The Jews could not deny it, although the proclamation of the resurrection of Jesus caused mayhem in the streets of Jerusalem. The Romans could not deny it, though it was the most embarrassing event in all the ten years of Pontius Pilate's prefecture of Judea. The tomb was empty. Why?

There are only two possibilities. It could be empty because someone stole the body or because God raised Jesus from the dead. There are no other options.

Right, let us go for the easier option first. Who would have wanted to remove the body of Jesus? His enemies? Hardly! They had been plotting night and day to put Him in that tomb. Now they had succeeded. They were not going to move His body. Not at any price. And if for any perverse reason they had done so, they would have been in a marvelous position to discredit the claims of the Christians once they started a near-revolution in Jerusalem by proclaiming the resurrection of Jesus. *They would only have needed to produce the body!* But that they could not do. And, incidentally, the tomb of Jesus never became a place of pilgrimage, as was the case with other dead heroes.

But could not His friends have moved the body? It seems attractive, at first sight. But it will not do. These disciples were transformed. They went all over the Mediterranean world preaching with might and main that God had raised Jesus from the dead. Would they have done that if they knew it was not true? Would they have faced torture and martyrdom (which actually befell many of them) if they knew it simply was not true that Jesus had risen from the dead? I think not. You can let yourself be killed for a mistake, maybe, but not for a fraud. It is simply inconceivable that the dynamic growth of the early church and its total lack of fear could have arisen from deceit. Besides, the disciples had cherished no expectation that Jesus would rise from the grave. And what is more, there was a guard on the tomb. It is very difficult to see how they could have raided the grave of Jesus even if they wanted to. And the Gospels make it very clear that they did not want to. Most of them simply wanted to save their skins by getting out from under this terrible Jesus fiasco. They fled back to Galilee. Fast.

Very well then. If Jesus was not removed from the tomb by either His friends or His enemies, what possibilities remain?

Only one. He was raised by God. And that is what every strand of the New Testament asserts.

There is one more delightful detail about the empty tomb of Jesus we must not miss. John's gospel tells us that it was Mary of Magdala who first met Jesus after the Resurrection. In shock she rushed back to the disciples and told them. Peter and John ran to the tomb. John got there first: he was the younger man. When Peter puffed up, he actually entered the tomb. It was empty, apart from the grave clothes of Jesus. And these were very significantly arranged. The strips of linen that had been wound around His body were in one place. The covering that had been around His head was in another. Do you see what that means? The grave clothes were undisturbed, but the body was gone — like a chrysalis case when the butterfly has emerged. No wonder the two disciples went home thinking furiously. The empty tomb was, and remains, a powerful indicator that Jesus was no longer dead but had somehow been raised to new life.

A Crowd of Witnesses

But the Christian faith in the resurrection of Jesus does not rest on an empty tomb. Far from it. That would be much the same as to say that we believe in butterflies because of empty chrysalis cases. We believe in butterflies because we see them. And that was the inestimable privilege of the first disciples of Jesus. They saw Him. They talked with Him, ate with Him, for a full forty days. They did not believe in His resurrection because the tomb was empty. They believed because they had personally encountered the risen Jesus. Sometimes it was in an upper room, like the one where they celebrated that last Passover together. Sometimes it was on a walk. Sometimes it was when they were gathered for prayer. Sometimes it was when they were out fishing. Jesus appeared to them in a variety of contexts. He taught them more about the kingdom of God and how they were to make it known. Those six weeks of companionship with the risen Jesus were conclusive. They *knew* He was alive. And, of course, it made such a difference to them. No longer were they embarrassed or terrified. They were full of confidence. You find them out on the streets telling all and sundry that Jesus was alive again and calling everybody to follow Him into the kingdom of God.

A New Community

And this leads us to one of the most powerful pieces of evidence for the Resurrection. The Christian church was born. It did not exist until about A.D. 30, and then, just as its leader was executed and His movement seemed extinguished, it suddenly burst into life and spread like wildfire. *Something* must have started it off. What can you suggest if not the resurrection of Jesus? Those first disciples had collapsed like a house of cards when Jesus was arrested. They had run away, some of them back home to Galilee. But now nothing can silence them. What is the cause of it — if not the resurrection of Jesus? This new movement had no finances behind it. It had no proven leadership. It had no experience. It had no education. It had no training in evangelism. Yet it turned ancient society upside down. It was the start of a movement that has changed the whole world. It was the start of a movement that survived the fall of the Roman Empire. It was the start of a movement that has penetrated every country on earth with the good news of Jesus and His love.

And this new movement had two powerful marks of membership. Neither of them makes any sense if Jesus did not rise from the dead. If He did, both make lots of sense.

First was baptism. Christian baptism is no social convenience. It is meant to be a symbolic incorporation into the death and resurrection of Jesus, no less. Hence the submersion into the waters; hence, too, the rising to new life as the candidate emerges. And baptism is the distinctive mark of the Christian. Do you see how this most basic badge of belonging is irrevocably linked not only to the death of Jesus but also to His resurrection?

The other innovation was Sunday, the Lord's Day as they called it. Jews had, from time immemorial, kept Saturday sacred to mark God's completion of His work of creating the world. They would not work on this day. They would not fight. It was for worshiping God. If God Himself had rested from His labors of creation, then His people should rest, too. And passionate Jews though they all were, these first believers in Jesus were so convinced of the reality and importance of the Resurrection that they managed in due time to change the day of rest from Saturday to Sunday. That was a monumental achievement. Just you try changing the day of rest from Sunday to Monday and see how far you get! Yet the early Christians succeeded. Why? Because something totally new, totally unheard-of had taken place. Jesus had risen from the dead on Sunday, the first Easter Day. They simply had to celebrate it. It was the most wonderful thing that had ever happened.

When you consider the matter coolly, the birth, survival, and growth of the Christian church are immensely strong pointers to the truth of the Resurrection. This faith has more adherents than any other in the world. They are to be found in every nation under the sun. Instead of diminishing as the years roll on, they expand. They are not held together by any external structures. They have no binding rules. It is a perfectly astonishing story. And when you look a little closer and take note of the persecution that has so often engulfed the church, the corruption that has so often brought it into disrepute, the failure that has so often overtaken it, the intrigue that has so often disgraced it — when you think of all this, does it not seem to you that the living Christ must be there somewhere, giving it life, or it would have folded up centuries ago? If any business were run with the inefficiency of the church, it would not last a year in the marketplace, would it? And yet the gospel grows and spreads. Jesus foretold that the gates of hell would never prevail against His church. They never have. They never will. For the living Jesus holds it in His hand.

A Radical Transformation

But it is not just the fact of the church's existence and spread that fascinates me as I look at this issue of the Resurrection. It is the changed lives of real people who come into contact with the risen Jesus. Take, for example, two of the people I have met tonight. One is a lady with multiple sclerosis. She drives around in a little buggy. Her life is unimaginably curtailed from what it used to be. She has to have most things done for her. But she shines. There is no other word for it. She shines with the reflected light of Jesus. It is very obvious and very wonderful. She does not just know *about* Him: she *knows* Him. The other is a businessman who was very successful in his job and pretty disastrous in the areas of marriage and alcohol and the like. He met with Jesus Christ, and it has made a totally new man of him. No drink now. A fine marriage. A remarkable ministry in the world of young offenders, heading an organization that be-friends youngsters in prison, helps them when they come out, and sees many of them turn to Christ. He has just returned from Japan, speaking of Christ to other businessmen there, men with similar problems to the ones he had. They began to realize that this was not just another *religion*: it was a *relationship* with the living Christ, and there is nothing like it in all the world.

Those just happen to be people I came across tonight. But it is happening all the time. Jesus proves His resurrection not so much by arguments in a book as by lives that He takes and reshapes as they enter into this relationship with Him. It has always been like that. The earliest surviving record of the resurrection of Jesus was written by the apostle Paul early in the fifties of the first century to the Christians at Corinth. He says,

> I delivered to you as of first importance what I also received, that Christ died for our sins in accordance with the scriptures, that he was buried, that he was raised on the third day in accordance with the scriptures, and that he appeared to Cephas, then to the twelve. Then he appeared to more than five hundred brethren at one time, most of whom are still alive, though some have fallen asleep. Then he appeared to James, then to all the apostles. Last of all, as to one untimely born, he appeared also to me (1 Cor. 15:3–8).

Notice two things about that remarkable testimony. First, it is astonishingly early. Paul reminds his Corinthian friends that the stories of the risen Jesus he told them when he brought them the gospel a few years earlier, he had himself learned after his conversion, which occurred only two or three years after the Resurrection itself. It was the resurrection of Jesus that made Paul a Christian: he met with Jesus personally on the road to Damascus. And he attests the truth of these encounters of the risen Christ with various people whom he mentions in this excerpt. That is wonderful, early, firsthand evidence.

But the main thing here is the life-changing power of Jesus, is it not? Look how Jesus changed the Twelve from a dispirited rabble into a task force. Look how He rescued Cephas (the old Aramaic name for Peter) from despair and made him the leader of the earliest church. Look how He appeared to more than five hundred disciples and turned them into a church. Look how He turned James, a member of His own family circle, from an uncommitted skeptic to a respected Christian disciple who was called on to lead the Jerusalem church. Look how He appeared to "all the apostles," including Thomas, and changed him from a hard-nosed pessimist into an ardent worshiper. Look how He changed Saul of Tarsus, the most dangerous enemy the earliest church had, into the greatest missionary teacher the world has ever known. It is the impact of the risen Jesus that did all that! It still happens today.

A Host of Implications

The implications of all this are enormous.

If Jesus really did rise from the dead, we can be very sure that He was who He claimed to be. There is an old scrap of a creed preserved in the New Testament, which puts it very clearly:

> [He] was descended from David according to the flesh and designated Son of God . . . by his resurrection from the dead (Rom. 1:3–4).

The Resurrection is the capstone on His claims.

If Jesus really did rise from the dead, we can be sure that the job He did of lifting the burden of the world's sin on the cross was complete and finished. Listen to Paul on the subject:

> He was delivered up to death because of our offenses, and he was raised to life again because we have been acquitted (Rom. 4:25).

If Jesus really did rise from the dead, we can be sure that there is such a thing as life after death, and that He is equipped to lead us there. We need no longer speculate about whether or not we live on after we die. Jesus has gone behind the death barrier and returned to show that a new life awaits His followers. He promised that "in my Father's house are many rooms" (John 14:2), and His resurrection proved it.

If Jesus really did rise from the dead, we can be profoundly optimistic about the future of humankind. The future does not lie with the nuclear bomb or with ecological disaster. It lies in the hands of the risen Lord of the universe. What cause for joy!

If Jesus really did rise from the dead, that accounts for these changed lives we have been talking about because the very same power that raised Jesus from the tomb is available to raise His followers from various deaths and bondages in which they are themselves entangled. He lives to set us free.

If Jesus really did rise from the dead, if He has been raised to a new and deathless quality of life, the most momentous consequence of all is this: *He is still around!* I still recall the force with which this struck me at the time I was beginning to become a disciple of His. If He rose, He must be alive. If He is alive, why should I not meet with Him?

And I did. That's how I became sure. Read on: it can happen to everyone.

CHAPTER NINE

~

Can We Meet Him?

There are lots of people who would be able to follow along with this book so far. They believe Jesus was a real person. They believe His teaching and His mighty acts. They believe He died on the cross. They believe that He rose again from the dead. But somehow it isn't real. Somehow He is still the Stranger of Galilee to them.

You often find them in church circles, curiously enough. Ask someone if he or she is a Christian and the reply may be, "Yes, I believe in God" or "I was brought up Catholic" or "I go to church." But ask people if they know Jesus for themselves, and they will be surprised, sometimes annoyed. That sort of thing is for the "born again" brigade, the religious nut cases.

What has happened, it seems to me, is this. There is a widespread and fundamental misunderstanding of what Christianity is. Most people think it is a *religion*. Actually it is a *relationship*. It is not a once-a-week chore, not a matter of standards to keep up, of buildings to maintain, of the right clothes to wear, of services to attend. No. Those things do not bring us anywhere near the heart of Christianity. The heart of the whole thing is a personal relationship with Jesus, the most wonderful, attractive person who has ever lived. He is, as we saw in the last chapter, very much alive and well. He can be met. And if we have not met Him yet, we haven't lived.

Well, you say, that's all very well, but how could I meet Him?

How would you have met up with Him if you had been a contemporary of His in Galilee? It is not so very different today.

You Hear the News

First, you would have heard about Him, no doubt. He was news. You would have had friends who had been influenced by Him. You would have gotten from them some scraps of His teaching but, more important, some flavor of the Man Himself. And you would want to know more. This is eminently right and precisely what we should do today. Prick up your ears when one of your friends tells you that Jesus has made a real difference in his or her life. Don't immediately set up your defense mechanisms. Cultivate an open and inquiring mind on the subject. After all, if it is true, it is too good to miss.

You Check Him Out

Second, had you lived in the first century you would have set about checking Jesus out. You would listen to His teaching. You would reflect on His images of the kingdom being like a treasure hidden in a field or a pearl of great price. You would realize how true and how attractive it all was. You would hear Him talk of your life as if you lived in a house captured by a bandit who held you in bondage until someone bigger and tougher throws him out and brings you much-needed freedom. You might catch a whiff of the camaraderie of the disciples, their joy in the company of Jesus and of one another, and be a bit wistful.

It is just the same for us. There are two main ways of checking Jesus out these days, separated as we are by many centuries from when He walked the streets of Palestine. First, get hold of one or more of the Gospels in a modern translation, and read it as if you had never read it before. And as you do so, breathe a prayer, maybe something like this—just to show God you are not playing games but you really want to find out:

O God, if You are really there, show me what is true in this gospel that I am going to read. And I promise that I will follow the truth wherever it leads me—even if it is into the Christian camp, which I rather dread.

That is one great way of checking Jesus out. Go for the basic documents, and read them with an open mind. The other way is to get alongside some of His followers, people who say they know Him and He has made changes in their lives. You probably know such people. There are lots of them around. Watch their life-style. Talk to them. Go to worship with them. See if it all begins to make sense. It's a bit as if you were checking a doctor when you come to live in a new town. One way would be to look through his references and qualifications. The other would be to ask his patients, "Is he any good?" So look at the Gospels, and look at His followers. Of course they will have lots of failing: He hasn't finished reshaping them yet. But is there a real change that can credibly be attributed to Jesus? And does their worship have a ring of truth about it? Christians show their loving adoration for their Lord in a variety of styles. Some churches seem rather stagnant. But you will know others in your neighborhood where this is far from the case, churches with a practical concern for their area, with a reality in their worship, with a love in their congregation. Go and try out a church like that. It is all part of the search.

You Count the Cost

Third, if you had lived in the days of Jesus, you would need to count the cost of following Him. He said that if you were going to follow Him, it would mean giving Him priority over family, friends, and job. Following Him would call for perseverance: it would never do to start building and then find you did not have the resources to go on. It would mean facing opposition. Jesus said it would be like going out to war. What's more, it would mean being in a minority in that war. Can you face going out with ten thousand to face an army of twenty thousand? You are bound to meet opposition if you live for Christ, and you are bound to be in a minority unless you live in some Bible belt!

Jesus was very radical. He said, "Whoever . . . does not renounce all that he has cannot be my disciple" (Luke 14:33). He did not mean that they should go out and sell all they had. His disciples retained their homes and their fishing boats. But He did mean that they should no longer consider themselves as the *owners* of anything they had—just the *tenants*. Jesus would be Number One from that time on. The true disciple has no possessions kept hidden from his Master.

So to follow Him would be a very costly decision. It would need to be most carefully considered. But then so would the alternative. What would it cost to miss the kingdom of God? How terrible to have turned your back on the best news ever. How terrible to have built the whole of your life on sand instead of on the rock of Jesus, sand that simply could not withstand the storms and tides of life. And eternity—the first-century inquirer would recall that nobody in all the history of Israel had ever spoken so seriously and so much about heaven and hell as Jesus did. The choice is real. It is inescapable.

So it would be very important to count the cost. And it still is. Jesus wants to come before family, job, ambitions. He wants to be not a hobby for Sundays but the driving force of your whole life—Number One, no less. Can you face it? Are you willing to take Jesus not simply as Savior but as Lord and Master? Is it worth it?

As you ponder that question, think of the joy His friendship can bring not only in good times but in bad, not only in this life but in the next.

Think of the strength of His character, and the difference that moral power could make if you allowed it access to your life.

Think of the forgiveness He offers, forgiveness you can find nowhere else in the world.

Think of the purpose and zest it gives to life when you invest it for Jesus and His kingdom.

Think of the calm and peace He can bring in the pressures of life.

Think, too, of the amazing companionship and depth of relationship there is between real brothers and sisters in the family of God worldwide. There's no club to match it!

Consider these things carefully, and ask yourself if it is worth missing all that, missing what you were made for? It is costly to follow Jesus. That is certain. But it is even more costly to turn your back on Him. You have to make up your mind, one way or the other, and then live with your decision. You can't even contract out by doing nothing: not to decide *is* to decide!

You Face the Implications

Fourth, the first-century contemporary of Jesus would have been bound to pause once more before committing himself. The claims of Jesus were so very final. He was the Bread of Life, not one of many bakers. He was the Way to God, not one of many guides. He was the Life of God, not one of many ethical advisers. He was the Truth, not one of many teachers. How hard that was to accept in the first century! How hard today. How could this carpenter make such outrageous claims?

Well, the trouble is that His authoritative teaching, His matchless character, and His undeniable miracles all back up those claims. The whole package hangs together. And His death and resurrection only served to underline it. There never has been and never will be anyone like Jesus. The ideal has lived.

That is not for a moment to put down other religious teachers. It simply points us away from the partial to the complete, from the good to the best. There were many good rabbis in Palestine in Jesus' day. There was much that was good in the temple and synagogue worship, in the teachings, the prayers, and the sacrifices. But if you were to become a follower of Jesus, you would necessarily have to give Him priority over these good but incomplete ways of worshiping God. That was unpopular. It still is.

Coming to Jesus in these days of rampant pluralism is like getting married. You may have flirted with all kinds of spirituality — cults, other faiths, even self-deification. But now you are going to make a lasting and exclusive commitment. In Jesus alone you will discover God as Father. In Jesus alone will you find the One who on the cross took responsibility for your failures and rebellion. Jesus alone rose from the tomb: no other religious leader has ever done that. Jesus alone can put His unseen Spirit inside your very being. The time has come to put your whole life in His hand.

How do you do that?

You Come to Him

How did you do it in the first century? You would have come to Him and told Him that you were unworthy to enter the kingdom of God but were going to respond to His wonderful free invitation. You would need to tell Him that your life was far from what you would like it to be: you would have been a rebel against the heavenly Father. But now you are coming home. And Jesus would welcome you. Did He not say, "Come to me, all who labor and are heavy laden, and I will give you rest" (Matt. 11:28)? Yes, He would welcome you. And then He would invite you publicly to align yourself with His cause and smilingly invite you, "Come. Follow Me." And you would start to do just that. Interestingly enough, you would find that the decision that seemed so hard before you made it looked so obvious in retrospect. You would find that the discipleship that seemed so awesome beforehand was so fulfilling once you had begun.

And that is precisely how you come to Jesus today. You simply talk to Him. It may seem very strange talking when it feels as if there is no one there to answer. But there is Someone there, although you cannot see Him. That is where faith comes in. You trust that there is Someone there (and it is like assuming a certainty because this is no vague spiritual force you are addressing, but the historical Jesus who lived and died and rose again). And you say to Him in your own words something like this:

> Jesus, I am amazed that You should bother about me and love me and want me to be Your friend and disciple. I know that there is a lot in my life that needs cleaning up. Please come and do it. I still have lots of questions that bother me, but I lay them all before You in the tangle that they are. I do believe that You went to the cross for me to deal with my guilty past. And I do believe that You are alive again. You invite people to come to You. And I'm coming. I'm coming now.

A prayer of surrender like that is all that is needed in order to meet Jesus and begin to discover that He is real. The Gospels call it repentance and faith. Repentance means turning away from the wrong things that have captured and dazzled you. Faith means turning to Jesus. It's a complete about turn. And you have just done it, as best you know how. Fortunately it is not a matter of technique, of saying the right things. It is a matter of the heart, of really wanting Jesus to come and start changing you.

You Handle Doubt

Most people find that after making this commitment, they are assailed by doubt. So be forewarned and forearmed. Meet the inevitable doubts of the early days with some promise of Jesus that means a lot to you. Perhaps one like this:

Him who comes to me I will not cast out (John 6:37).

You have come to Him, right? Then you have His word for it that He will never throw you out. Say that promise over and over again until you have it by heart. When I first reached out and discovered Jesus was real, I found particular encouragement in His words at the very end of Matthew's gospel:

I am with you always, to the close of the age.

That meant so much to me. He undertook to stay with me always, even when I failed Him, forgot Him, and let Him down. Amazing! Hang on to some of the promises of Jesus. They are an enormous encouragement as you start out.

Remember, too, when doubts come, that Jesus dealt with your failures and sins on that mysterious cross. And He cried out that it was finished. The job was done. It never needs to be repeated. Be very clear about that. Your confidence as a Christian will be strongly affected by it. Because when you do something wrong, as we all do, a little voice will whisper to you, "There, it isn't any good. You have gone and done it again. And I thought you were supposed to be a Christian!" That is one of the devil's prime ploys. Don't be taken in by it. Reply, "Yes, I admit I have done it again. And I am heartily ashamed. I have already apologized to my Lord about it. But He dealt decisively with all its evil consequences on the cross. So you cannot shake my confidence. I am relying on what He has done, and I shall get up and go on — a wiser disciple."

You Enter a New World

The New Testament tells us that a whole new world begins to open up once we enter the kingdom by surrendering to the King. The "newness" comes to different people in different ways. Some people have a great sense of relief: they have done what has been hanging over them for ages, and it feels so good. Others experience a gentle joy and the assurance that they are welcomed by God. Others are struck by a deep sense of peace, that the right thing has been done and that all is well. Others begin to find the companionship of Jesus a reality right from the start. Others discover some notable initial encouragement. With me it was obscene language, in which I was totally enmeshed: it fell away immediately. Some people receive a special gift of language they do not understand that helps them in prayer; the New Testament calls it the gift of "tongues." Most people find that prayer begins to become a reality, and they find themselves doing it at all sorts of odd moments. For many, too, the company of other Christians begins to become congenial: indeed, something we feel we cannot do without. We are in the family now, and we need our brothers and sisters.

And sometimes people feel nothing at all!

I cannot emphasize too strongly that it is perfectly all right to feel nothing at all to begin with. God has promised to accept you if you entrust yourself to Him. He has not promised you all kinds of feelings. These may or may not be present. If He chooses to give some mark of His acceptance, such as one of those I have outlined above, fine. If not, that is fine, too. You are brought into His kingdom not by your feelings but by Jesus. He has promised that He will never reject the person who comes to Him. And you have come. So He *has* accepted you. You have His word on this matter.

There is no more to be said. In due course there will be new joy and peace and power and fellowship and confidence — in some measure. These are kingdom gifts. But they don't all come at once or in any particular order. God does not deal with us *en masse* but individually. Our salvation is handcrafted! Once you have given in to Him, Jesus will steal up on you and assure you that He is real and that you have indeed met with Him. But He will do it in His own time and in His own way. Keep your eyes open for it!

CHAPTER TEN

~

What About the Church?

If I entrust my life to Jesus, you may well be thinking, *how does that place me within the church?* A whole group of problems, arising from our experiences of the church, our background, and our prejudices, combine to make this a confusing and perhaps somewhat alarming question for some. Others found the church before Jesus became a reality to them, so for them there is little problem. They had the frame before. Now they have the picture. But the link between Jesus and the church is one that we cannot avoid as we draw this book to an end.

Did Jesus Anticipate the Church?

Did Jesus ever expect the church to emerge? That is a question to which scholars have given different answers. One of them wittily observed that Jesus went about preaching the kingdom of God and all that emerged was the church! When you look into the matter, that judgment is more amusing than true.

What is absolutely certain is that Jesus had no time for purely individual religion. Real repentance and faith brought you into a kingdom, into a family. There was a sense of belonging. It is fair to say that the Christianity that does not begin with the individual does not begin, but the Christianity that ends with the individual ends. The way to Christ may seem, and often is, a lonely and very personal journey. But as soon as you have gone through the narrow gate of repentance, you find yourself part of a joyful, jostling crowd.

And that Jesus certainly anticipated.

For one thing, He deliberately chose twelve of the disciples to be His "apostles," His delegates. That number was highly significant. It was the counterpart to the twelve tribes of Israel. Indeed, Jesus says that His twelve disciples will, one day, judge the twelve tribes of Israel. For another, Jesus twice speaks of the church. In one place He tells Peter (who has just come out with the tremendous assertion that Jesus is the Messiah, the Son of the living God) that on this rock He will build His church and the powers of hell will not prevail against it (see Matt. 16:17–19). A very significant statement. For the Messiah was never conceived, in Jewish thought, without His messianic community. And although, as we have seen, Jesus did not Himself choose the title *Messiah*, when Peter did use it, Jesus took it a stage further and included the community over which the Messiah would preside. He called it "my church." He guards it. It is entered by relationship with Him. It will never fade away. The gates of hell will not prevail against it. It is the community that He calls into being, that He leads, and that will continue His work after His death and resurrection.

The other reference is equally interesting. Jesus is teaching His disciples how to settle disputes in the future. If your brother offends you, go and tell him his fault personally, He says. If he won't listen, take two or three people along as witnesses. If he won't listen to them, make the matter known to the church. If he will not listen to the church, he has forfeited his place within the church. He must be treated like an outsider (see Matt. 18:15–20). This shows clearly that Jesus did foresee the church that would emerge after His death and resurrection. It was no mistake. He saw it as the Christian community to which they would all belong. He anticipated that it would have a disciplinary role.

Yes, there is no doubt that Jesus anticipated the church, and that the church was part of His purpose. Of course, we cannot peer into His mind. If I might hazard a guess, I would imagine that Jesus, as He proclaimed the kingdom of God, hoped that no new society would be necessary because all Israel would press gladly into the kingdom. But the reception He got from the rulers of His country bred the realistic recognition that not all Israel would accept the free invitation of God, and that therefore a new community would be needed, a community of those who did acknowledge God's kingship in their lives and were bound together in total surrender to His Son. And this thought seems to have grown in Him as the storm clouds of opposition gathered and as His end inexorably drew near.

He spoke of those followers of His as a "little flock" to whom it was the heavenly Father's pleasure to give the kingdom. He saw Himself as God's vine and His followers as branches in that vine — an undeniably corporate image. He saw Himself as God's temple where worship should be made and His followers as stones in that temple. He saw Himself as God's Good Shepherd and His disciples as sheep. You simply cannot get away from the corporate nature of the discipleship into which Jesus was calling people. He did not come to save souls. The New Testament never speaks like that. He came to bring into being a new community, a foretaste of the kingdom of God, and an appetizer for heaven.

What Did Jesus Want the Church to Be?

How did He hope the church would turn out?

We are fortunately not left in doubt about that. We have in the seventeenth chapter of John's gospel a record of the remarkable prayer that Jesus prayed on the evening before His trial and death. It is mainly about the church. Let me outline what Jesus was praying for, what He was longing for, in His church. Here are the marks of the church, as Jesus saw them. It is a perfectly astonishing list.

The church consists of people who know God and Jesus whom He has sent: not just know *about* Him, *know Him*. And that, says Jesus, is to have already here and now the life that will last forever.

The church consists of people who set out to glorify Him, just as He glorifies His heavenly Father. A deep word, *glorify*. It's all to do with light. And it means letting the sheer brilliance of God's radiance be reflected in the way you live. Just as the moon reflects the glory of the sun, so the church is meant to reflect the glory of the Lord so that people can look at Christians and exclaim, "There's something different about those people."

The church consists of people who keep His word. By this Jesus means that those who observe His teaching revere it and try to obey it rather than find ways of circumventing its challenge.

The church consists of people who genuinely believe that Jesus came from God and that God sent Him for His unique mission. He was not only a great teacher. Christians are meant to have clear views about Jesus.

The church consists of people who are united, in the same way as Jesus is united with His heavenly Father. That unity does not necessarily mean uniformity, but it does mean identity of purpose, mutual love, and recognizable belonging. Christian unity in this sense is not a secondary issue. It is absolutely vital. Jesus says that nothing less than the love, trust, and mutual belonging of the church will convince people that God loves them and has sent Jesus for their rescue.

The church consists of people who live their ordinary lives in the world but are sustained by God. Not hermits, taken out of the world. Not worldlings, submerged in it. But ordinary people displaying the extraordinary power and love and protection of God in their lives.

The church consists of people who have the same sort of joy as Jesus had. This is perfectly compatible with sorrow and loneliness at times. But it is the governing emotion of Christians' lives. Why not, if God loves them and has died for them? It can't be all that bad if that is the case, can it? Christians have something to sing about.

The church consists of people who can face the music. People who will stick to their guns even when the going is rough. The world will hate them, just as it hated Jesus. They are called to endure, as He endured. That is one of the marks of the true church of God.

The church consists of people whose home and priorities are not bounded by this world. They are, in a sense, aliens and exiles here, as Jesus was. That does not mean they will not throw all their weight into changing and improving society. They will. But they know that this world is not all there is. It is not their final home.

The church consists of people who will deliberately set themselves apart from all they know to be wrong in order to be of service to their friends and acquaintances who are as yet strangers to Jesus. He Himself did that for all of us. He expects to see that attitude mirrored in His followers.

The church consists of people who do not sit comfortably in

church on Sunday and then wait for a repeat performance next week but are sent out into the world, as Jesus was sent by His heavenly Father, to bring God's healing to needy and hurting people.

The church consists of people who model His love, the love that pours itself out on the undeserving. Such love is the mark of the followers of Jesus. This is how they are to be known.

The church consists of people in whom Jesus Himself lives. They are not copying Him, strictly speaking. They are allowing His unseen presence — what he called His Holy Spirit — to come and live in them and allowing His fragrance to flow from them. The idea is that people should look at the church and immediately be made aware of and attracted to Jesus.

And finally, the church consists of people who will share the home of Jesus with His heavenly Father for all eternity. That is their destiny. Nothing less.

The Vision — and the Reality

What an incredible vision of what the church ought to be and might be! And what an incredible anticlimax the church as we see it today, and as it has displayed itself throughout history, has proved to be. But the lovely thing is that Jesus has not given up on the church. He does not propose to scrap it. The powers of hell will never prevail against it. For it is His church. He brought it into being. He lives in it. He is at work purifying and guiding it. There is no reason for discouragement, let alone despair. Why, the church is a colony of heaven, and we are told that Christ loved the church and gave Himself for it. He will not abandon it.

And you and I are members of that worldwide church if we have surrendered our lives to Jesus and been baptized into the fellowship. The church is not the kingdom of God — thank goodness! If it were, I think I should bow out. No, the church is only a tiny part of God's kingly rule in this world. But it is the part of His kingdom that, theoretically at least, recognizes His rule and attempts to abide by it. The part of the church we belong to is not, I suspect, of supreme importance.

The church is an army that marches under many banners. Our regiment in that army will be determined to some extent by our background, to some extent by our understanding, and to some extent by our temperament. No, it is not of supreme importance what regiment we belong to. What is of supreme importance is that we pay attention to our Commanding Officer and that we do not find fault with other regiments in the same army, but do our utmost to understand and allow for their strange regimental customs because we realize that the things that unite us in the kingdom of God are so much more important than the things that divide.

How Can We Be His Disciples?

Very well then. Let's be practical. How can we play our part in this community of Jesus, which He left to continue His work on earth? Or to put it another way, how can we in the twentieth century be the disciples of Jesus as the Twelve were, along with many others, in the first century? Well, the Gospels make it plain that there are certain important characteristics in real disciples.

First, disciples are *chosen*. They may think they have chosen Jesus, but actually He has chosen them and called them, and they have merely responded to that call. The initiative has rested with Him. And what a relief that is. When the heat is on, what a joy to think that Jesus has chosen you, even you. When you have failed, what an encouragement to know that He has chosen you. When you are successful, what a joy to know that it is not your brilliance that has produced that result. You are simply doing what the Master has chosen for you. It is a wonderful ground of assurance. "You have not chosen me," He once told His disciples, "but I have chosen you and sent you to bear fruit" (see John 15:16).

Second, disciples *spend time* with the Master. When Jesus chose the Twelve, we read that He chose them "to be with him, and to be sent out to preach" (Mark 3:14). Note the order. The "being with him" is indispensable. You see, Jesus does not want a bunch of robots who go out and work for Him. He wants what C. S. Lewis once called, with great daring, "little Christs" who would know Him, love Him, and be a bit like Him. So that is where prayer comes in. Top of the list. There are a lot of different sides to prayer: asking for things, thanking for things, praising God for who He is, just being silent in His presence, confessing our failures. Yes, all of that. But the heart of it is *being together* with Jesus. Fathers and sons love that togetherness. Mothers and daughters love it. Lovers thrive on it. Christians, too, revel in it. Time apart with Jesus is fundamental to growth in discipleship. Make room for it in a regular, scheduled way every day.

Third, disciples *learn* from the Master. That is what a disciple is, a learner. In the days when He was on earth they listened to every word He spoke. They did not always understand or obey. But they knew they were learners. And it is just the same today. We cannot hear His voice in person. But we have the substance of His teaching, the Gospels. We need to feed on those Gospels. We need to take their message to heart — along with the Old Testament, which preceded them, and the letters of the New Testament, which follow them. One of the great weaknesses of the church today is that ordinary Christians do not normally read their Bibles on a regular basis and do not make the teaching of Jesus decisive for the way they view ecology, taxes, marriage and divorce, abortion, and other pressing social and personal issues. We would not think much of an embassy that knew little of its country's policies. Yet the church is often such an embassy today. If we mean business as disciples, we will make time (and it will mean *making* it) to read the Bible on a regular basis. Bible reading systems like the lectionary in the Book of Common Prayer, or Ligonier Ministries' "Table Talk." or Back to the Bible's "Our Daily Bread," or "Read Your Bible Through in a Year" found in many Nelson Bibles are a real help.

Fourth, disciples *share*. They share with each other their friendship for the Master. They share experiences together. To put it another way, disciples are not individualists, doing their own thing. They are trying to do Jesus' thing, and to do it together. That is why worship in church is so important. It is something we do to honor our Master together. That is why informal fellowship in the home, including Bible study, prayer times, unstructured worship, and the sharing of concerns, is so important. If you duck out of such fellowship, you will soon lose your joy in Jesus and your desire to grow. Fellowship is not a luxury. It is a necessity.

Fifth, disciples *follow*. They do what their Master tells them. There is a tough streak of obedience in the Christian life. It is not enough to hear good teaching on Sunday; we must do it. It is not enough to glorify God in our worship on Sunday; we must glorify Him from Monday to Saturday as well.

There are some very particular things that Jesus told us to do. He told us to be baptized as a mark both of His choice of us and of our choice of Him. Baptism is not an optional extra. He told us to break bread and drink wine as His memorial and to go on doing it until He comes again. The Communion is not an optional extra. Indeed, both baptism and Communion are tremendous encouragements to us: they are distinctive marks of Christian discipleship as well as means of drawing on His gracious strength.

But there are other things that Jesus specifically told us to do. He told us to love one another as He had loved us. He even told us to love our enemies. He told us not to judge one another. If we are disciples, we must take note of these commands and seek to carry them out. That is how we show our discipleship, and that is how it grows in depth and reality.

Sixth, disciples *work*. They are there to assist in their Master's enterprise. They are not drones in the hive of Jesus, but workers. One of the glories of the Christian church is this: you cannot really be a Christian without having a ministry. All Christians are called to serve. The shape of the service will be varied. How dull it would be otherwise! We are all called to work for Jesus. And the wonderful thing is that as we work for Him, so we grow, and our love for Him becomes deeper, our conviction about His truth becomes more settled, and our competence increases.

One of the great things that He expects from us is to be His witnesses. Notice I did not say His preachers. Not everyone is called to preach — thank goodness! But we are all called to bear witness to Jesus in our own words when opportunity offers. Think of a witness in a court of law. He does not preach. He does not tell the jury what to do. He simply tells what he saw or experienced. And that is such a powerful thing. If more Christians made a habit of unashamedly telling others of the difference Jesus has made in their lives, a great many more people would consider Christ and come to Him.

But of course we can work for Christ in so many other ways. Some will, for His sake, get involved in famine relief, others in working for human rights, others in politics, others in prison reform, and so on. There are so many dark places in this world where the light of Jesus needs to be shone by His followers. There is plenty of work to do, and the wise disciple is the one who prays, "Lord, what do You want me to do and to be for You?" It is our responsibility to pray like that for guidance. It is His responsibility to guide us.

And finally, disciples *please* their Master. Their supreme aim is to please Him. That is the purpose Jesus set Himself. Isn't that both a delightful and a liberating goal for you and me? Here are two lovers. How will they keep their love bright and constant? Why, by each setting themselves to please the other. You lose yourself, only to find it in the good of the other. Paradoxical, but true. And that is how the Christian disciple tries to act. There is not a whole rigmarole of rules and regulations governing behavior in the kingdom. The King asks us to please Him. Just that. And if we make that our aim, we shall do well. In ninety-nine cases out of a hundred, one has only to ask, "Lord, what would You like me to do?" for the answer to be abundantly plain. Perhaps our highest calling, as well as our deepest joy, is to try always to please the Lord who has set His love upon us and poured His Spirit into our hearts.

Such is the calling of the Christian community.

The Minus — and the Plus

There are two great differences between the first disciples and ourselves. We are at a disadvantage compared with them because we do not have the chance of listening to Jesus personally as a physical being among us. But we are at a great advantage compared with them in another respect. Jesus promised that the Holy Spirit, His own unseen self, would come and actually reside in His disciples after He had died and risen again. While He was on earth the Holy Spirit was concentrated within the person and expressed in the acts and words of Jesus. But once He had died and risen to a life that death could never again touch, His physical person returned to heaven. His presence could then be spiritually disseminated in the hearts of all who would have Him.

This is not something any of us can fully understand. Mercifully it is something that all real Christians have experienced from the Day of Pentecost onward. A Christian is someone who has the Spirit of Jesus living inside him or her. When we come to Jesus in repentance and faith, He not only welcomes us but puts His Spirit within us. And that Spirit guides us, encourages us, teaches us, strengthens us. It is like having Jesus not only alongside us, as the first disciples had, but inside us, as they did not have — until Pentecost.

So as we contemplate the calling of the church, its many failings, and our task as disciples, let us take heart. The very Spirit that dwelt in Jesus dwells in us. The very power that raised Him from the tomb is released in our lives. To follow Him is not only desirable; it is possible! And it is earth's greatest joy. Don't miss it.

Footnotes for the Curious

~

CHAPTER ELEVEN

Jesus: What Is the Secular Evidence?

Despite the widespread ignorance about Jesus, and the skepticism with which many regard supernatural claims made for Him, Jesus of Nazareth remains history's most intriguing figure. There is no shortage of new films and books about Him, and many of them are bizarre. It accords well with modern predilections to make Jesus elope with Mary Magdalene, to assert that He never died on the cross, that He was a counterculture rebel, a homosexual, and a second-century A.D. leader of the revolution against the bourgeois establishment. He has been seen as the cult figure at the center of a group who got high on hallucinogenic mushrooms. And needless to say, it has been suggested that He was a mythical figure who never existed.

None of these claims can be sustained without the most blatant disregard of the evidence. It may surprise some that there is a good deal of evidence, Christian and non-Christian, which enables us to get a bold, consistent picture of this astonishing figure Jesus. What follows is some of the non-Christian evidence about Him.

Greco-Roman

First, the evidence from early Roman writers. There is not a great deal of it. You would not expect wealthy men of letters in Rome to take a lot of note of a young carpenter who lived for a few years in Judea, on the edge of the map. What there is, however, is fascinating.

Tacitus, the great historian of the early empire, writing in A.D. 115, gives a careful account of leading events under each emperor on a year-by-year basis. When he gets to A.D. 64, the year when much of Rome was burned to the ground, he makes it plain that he agrees with the generally held view that Nero was responsible because he wanted to redevelop a large area in the center of the city as his palatial residence:

> To dispel the rumour, Nero substituted as culprits and treated with the most extreme punishments, some people, popularly known as Christians, whose disgraceful activities were notorious. The originator of the name, Christ, had been executed when Tiberius was emperor by order of the procurator Pontius Pilate. But the deadly cult, though checked for a time, was now breaking out again not only in Judaea, the birthplace of this evil, but even throughout Rome where all nasty and disgusting ideas from all over the world pour in and find a ready following (*Annals* 15.44).

Obviously, Tacitus has no time for Christianity, but he is clear that Christians did not burn down Rome. He has a basic knowledge of the "originator of the name," Christ, who was born in Judea, lived in the reign of Tiberius (A.D. 14–37), was executed by Pilate (who governed the province A.D. 26–36), and had an extensive following that was well established in the capital of the empire by the sixties of that century. It so happens that Tacitus had good opportunity to be well informed about Christian origins, for in A.D. 112 he was made governor of Asia where Christians were numerous, and he had spent much of his life in the East.

He referred to them again in a lost book of his, *Histories*, of which an excerpt has been preserved by a later writer. In it Tacitus recognizes that Christianity began as a sect within Judaism, though by his time it was quite separate, and he tells us that the Roman general Titus hoped, by destroying the temple in Jerusalem in A.D. 70, to put an end to both Judaism and Christianity, on the theory that if you cut the root, the plant will soon wither! And if we think it odd that Tacitus should not have had more to say about Jesus, it is salutary to remember that much of his work is lost, and that he provides us with the only mention in secular literature of the existence of Pontius Pilate.

More comes from Tacitus's contemporary, Pliny the Younger, another man of letters who was sent in A.D. 112 to govern Bithynia in northern Turkey. He was rather a pathetic, bureaucratic figure who was always writing letters to the Emperor Trajan. He writes one long letter about the Christians. They were spreading like wildfire in his province. Christianity was becoming a social and economic problem: the pagan temples were closing down for lack of customers, the sacred festivals were becoming deserted, and the demand for sacrificial animals had ceased. Pliny executed those who admitted their Christian allegiance. But he had qualms about it. That is why he wrote to the emperor. He had discovered that nothing untoward was practiced in these meetings of Christians. Their whole guilt lay in refusing to worship the imperial statue and images of the gods, and in their habit of meeting on a fixed day (Sunday) to sing hymns to Christ as God (*quasi deo*). Their lives, he wrote, were exemplary. You would not find fraud, adultery, theft, or dishonesty among them. And at their common meal they ate food of an ordinary and innocent kind. That is, no doubt, an allusion to the fact that Christians spoke of "feeding on Christ" in the Holy

Communion; to the uninitiated it could sound like cannibalism. To be sure, Pliny tells us nothing about Jesus Himself, but he is clear that the "Jesus movement" is a major force in this upland province adjoining the Black Sea. This secular governor gives testimony to the quality of life of the Christians; their weekly worship of Christ as God; their unwillingness to accord that title to others, even the emperor; the innocence of their worship meetings; and their phenomenal spread (Pliny, *Letters*, 10.96).

Writers of the stature of Pliny and Tacitus make the historicity of Jesus certain and confirm some of the evidence we find laid out at much greater length in the Gospels.

There are other incidental references even earlier.

The Samaritan historian Thallus, who wrote in Rome about A.D. 52, regarded the crucifixion of Jesus as so significant that he included it in his history of the world and wanted to explain the darkness that fell when Jesus died on the cross as an eclipse of the sun.

A Syrian called Mara bar Serapion wrote a letter from prison in the seventies of the first century. It is preserved in the British Museum. He reflects on what is in store for those who have persecuted a wise man like him! What advantage, he asks, did the Athenians get from putting Socrates to death? Nothing but plague and famine. What advantage did the Jews get from executing their wise King? Nothing but the sacking of their city and the dispersion of their nation! That is an obvious reference not only to Jesus and His death but to His claim to be the King of the Jews. And Serapion, remember, was no Christian.

Jewish Evidence

Judaism, too, has given us some evidence about Jesus. The Jewish guerrilla commander, Flavius Josephus, who led contingents in the war against Rome between A.D. 66 and 70, subsequently turned historian and wrote to try to restore the reputation of his countrymen in Roman eyes. He tells us a lot about names we find in the Gospels — the Herods, Caiaphas, John the Baptist, even James "the brother of Jesus, the so-called Christ." But most significant of all is his extended reference to Jesus Himself. It is worth quoting in full:

> And there arose about this time [he means Pilate's time as governor, A.D. 26–36] Jesus, a wise man, if indeed one should call him a man. For he was the performer of astonishing deeds, a teacher of those who are happy to receive the truth. He won over many Jews, and also many Greeks. He was the Christ (or Messiah). In response to a charge presented by the leading men among us, Pilate condemned him to the cross: but those who had loved him at first did not give up. For he appeared to them on the third day alive again, as the holy prophets had foretold, and had said many other wonderful things about him. And still to this day the race of Christians, named after him, has not died out (*Antiquities* 18.3.3).

Of course, such powerful attestation from so hostile a source as Josephus is amazing and has attracted enormous suspicion from those who simply cannot believe it is genuine. But it is in all the manuscripts of Josephus. It is as well attested as anything he wrote. No doubt some of it is sarcastic. "If indeed one should call him a man" might be a snide allusion to His divine claims. "He was the Christ" might allude to the charge affixed to His cross. But it remains a solid, textually reliable statement by Josephus (himself a late contemporary of Jesus) to the founder of Christianity, to His messiahship, His wisdom, His teaching, His miracles, His many conversions, His death, and His resurrection — not to mention the continuance of the movement.

There are more allusions to Jesus, direct and indirect, scattered among the writings of the rabbis. They originated after the break between Judaism and Christianity and are uniformly hostile. They allude to His birth, which was acknowledged to be *different*. Jesus is sometimes referred to as "Jeshua ben Panthera," which may reflect the Jewish libel that He was the product of an illegitimate union between Mary and a Roman soldier Pantheras or may be a corruption of the Greek word *parthenos* meaning "virgin." They allude to His miracles: "he practised magic and led Israel astray." They allude to His disciples, a close circle, one of whom was called Matthew. They allude to His death by crucifixion at Passovertide. They even allude to His claim to share the nature of God and to be returning in judgment at the end of history.

Archaeological Evidence

Archaeology joins Roman and Jewish sources in bearing some testimony to Jesus. A little house-church has been discovered in Herculaneum, a city destroyed, along with Pompeii, in August A.D. 79 by the massive eruption of Vesuvius. There are clear marks where a cross has been ripped off a wall, probably a precious possession that the owner wanted to rescue as he ran for his life. Christian inscriptions have been found in Pompeii, including the Rotas-Sator square, a fascinating acrostic of the opening words of the Lord's Prayer in Latin. The acrostic itself is a palindrome: it reads the same backward as forward. As it stands, it does not make much sense, yet it has been found in several early Christian locations and must therefore have been very important to them. It is arranged in the form of a square:

```
R      O      T      A      S
O      P      E      R      A
T      E      N      E      T
A      R      E      P      O
S      A      T      O      R
```

"Arepo the sower holds the wheels with care" is not very promising. But it is much more promising when rearranged as follows:

```
                    A

                    P
                    A
                    T
                    E
                    R
    A   PATERNOSTER   O
                    O
                    S
                    T
                    E
                    R

                    O
```

The implications of this are tremendous. It reflects the Lord's Prayer. God is hailed as Father, an unimaginable privilege. The cruciform shape emphasizes the centrality of the cross of Jesus. The repeated *A* and *O* (for Alpha and Omega, the first and last letters of the Greek alphabet) point to the cosmic significance of Jesus, as the origin and goal of the whole universe. And if this seems fanciful, note that everywhere you look in the Rotas-Sator square, the *T* is between the *O* and *A*. Now the Greek *T* was the emblem of the cross in the early church; after all, it looked like one. And the placing of the *T* between the *A* and *O* in each of the four occurrences reflects the Christian conviction that the cross of Jesus is the midpoint of all history. Is that not a remarkable find in several parts of the empire within a generation of the death of Jesus? It speaks volumes.

But that is not the only archaeological find of interest. We have a fascinating inscription from Nazareth. It is an imperial edict, and it calls down the death penalty on anyone who steals from tombs. The inscription belongs to the time of Tiberius (A.D. 14–37) or Claudius (A.D. 41–54). Bearing in mind its early date, its extreme penalty (grave robbers were not normally so harshly dealt with!), and its location in Jesus' hometown, it seems highly probable that this edict represents government reaction to the resurrection of Jesus. Pilate would have had to report the disappearance of the body of a "revolutionary leader." Emperors were very interested in such people! He would presumably have taken the line alluded to in Matthew 28:11ff., that the disciples of Jesus came and stole His body while the guard was asleep. Highly embarrassing — but not as embarrassing as admitting the Resurrection. We can well understand the sharpness of the imperial rejoinder.

Well known among archaeological discoveries is the repeated "fish" symbol. Its popularity among Christians was due to the five letters that make it up, each of which stands for a Greek word confessing their Christian belief. IXΘYS, *Ichthus*, is the Greek word for "fish," and Christians saw each of its letters standing for a word, i.e., *Iesous Christos Theou Huios Soter*, "Jesus Christ, Son of God, Savior." That was a succinct and very definite expression of Christian conviction, emanating from the earliest days of the church.

One of the most fascinating of all archaeological finds was discovered by the Israeli archaeologist, Professor Sukenik, in 1945. It was a sealed tomb, just outside Jerusalem, which had miraculously escaped being plundered. Its contents were intact. They included coins dating it to approximately A.D. 50, and five ossuaries, or bone caskets, now on display in Jerusalem. On two of these caskets the name of Jesus is clearly legible. One reads in Greek *Iesu Iou* (?Jesus, help) and the other in Aramaic *Yeshu' aloth* (?Jesus, let him arise). They are also clearly marked with charcoal crosses. I have seen them. They are very impressive. Of course, this find has sparked controversy, but Sukenik's own interpretation still seems the most probable, namely, that in these crudely scratched letters we have the earliest known allusion to Jesus by Christian believers. If so, the implications are staggering. They point to a Jesus who can bring help even when a loved one has died, and a Jesus who can raise the Christian dead to be with Him. And all within twenty years of the Resurrection itself!

Conclusion

Enough has been said, drawing on Roman, Jewish, and archaeological evidence, to show the historicity, the unusual birth, the teaching, the miracles, the disciples, the messianic claims, the crucifixion, the resurrection, and the promised return of Jesus at the end of history. Here we have the recognizable outline of the Jesus who meets us in the Gospels.

CHAPTER TWELVE

~

Jesus: Can We Trust the Gospels?

Most of what we know about Jesus comes from four small books called Gospels. The writers of the Gospels saw Jesus not as an isolated phenomenon but as the climax and fulfillment of God's dealing with the Jewish people. It is, therefore, important to establish whether or not we can rely on the picture of Jesus painted by these gospel writers. For should it turn out that the Gospels are a tissue of lies, we must face the fact that we have few other substantial records about Jesus. There simply is no other extensive early evidence. On the other hand, if we find that the Gospels are to be trusted, we shall find in them not only the picture of the greatest life ever lived but an implicit call to discipleship. Perhaps that is why we find it so hard to give them a dispassionate hearing.

There is another reason that makes it difficult for us. The Gospels come to us as part of the Bible, and the Bible is a strangely authoritative and "holy" book. We are ill-disposed to accept any absolute authorities these days, and the idea of an inspired writing given us by God, which we must obey, is not only strange to many of us, but offensive.

So let us be quite clear about this. I am not asking you to accept God's inspiration of the Gospels. Of course, many Christians, myself included, have come to the conclusion that God must have guided the authors, but nobody is being asked to start with that viewpoint. You and I simply want to know if we can give the Gospels the same sort of credit as we accord to a respected news correspondent in the *New York Times*. Do these gospel writers give us a reliable picture of their central figure and His significance?

What Are the Gospels?

First, what are the Gospels? More than 250 years of concentrated study have been lavished upon these slim documents by Christians, Jews, agnostics, and even atheists. It is universally agreed that the Gospels are an entirely new breed of literature. Nothing like them has appeared before or since. They are like a new eruption from the volcano of human creativity. They are not biographies of Jesus, showing, as they do, little interest in the details of His life. They are not histories, impinging, as they do, only slightly on world affairs of the day; they do not even give us a sequential account of Jesus' life. No, although they contain elements both of biography and of history, they constitute a new literary genre, *gospel*. That word, though occasionally used before, sprang into common use with Christianity.

It means "good news," and people applied it to what Christians *said* before using it of what they *wrote*. For Christians did not go about proclaiming a new religion, new duties, a new ideology. They proclaimed good news. Not about what man is called to do but about what God has done.

The first Christians believed, rightly or wrongly, that the life and death and raising to life again of their friend Jesus were the most important things that had ever happened, and they wanted to tell everybody about them. That accounts for the astonishing burst of missionary activity that marked the infant church. It also accounts for the confidence and Easter faith that mark nearly all the stories in the Gospels. The men who wrote them believed what they wrote. That does not mean they were unreliable or prejudiced. They were simply convinced and overflowing with their new discovery. And so very naturally *gospel* passed from being a spoken message to being a written account. And those written accounts about Jesus show us how the early missionaries preached Jesus.

That being so, it matters rather less who actually penned the Gospels. They each come to us not so much with a single author's personal authority, but as one man's condensation of the good news they were all busy preaching. There is a living community of faith behind each author. And the authors themselves were in close touch with the immediate disciples of Jesus and their circle.

Who Wrote Them, and When?

Of the four Gospels it is almost certain that Mark's was written first, probably in the sixties of the first century. Mark appears in the New Testament record as a close companion of both Peter and Paul. The early Christians tell us that he was the person who interpreted Peter's gospel preaching and made it available to a wide circle by writing it in a book. Of course, Mark would have gotten his material from several sources, but it is encouraging to know that his main informant was the man at the heart of it all, Simon Peter, the most famous of all Jesus' friends. Mark writes with a breathless urgency and enthusiasm, mainly about what Jesus did and how He met His death. It is very evidently preaching material put down on paper and has many vivid eyewitness touches that Mark would have heard from Peter's impassioned addresses.

Within a few years Matthew's gospel appeared. He wanted to help many Jews who were becoming followers of Jesus and to integrate them with the Greeks who were crowding into the church. He was a very organized writer and addressed himself primarily to the teachers and leaders in the new Christian community. We do not know exactly who this Matthew was who wrote the gospel. The early Christians thought he was Matthew the tax gatherer who became one of Jesus' disciples; but this is unlikely, if only because he uses Mark's gospel as his basic source. And it would be very odd for an eyewitness to draw from the record of someone who was not himself present! Probably the name of Matthew became associated with this gospel because it embodies a lot of special material he gathered. This was, most likely, the account of the many sayings of Jesus, absent from Mark, which also appear in Luke. Matthew, the tax gatherer, had ample opportunity to make a record of the sayings of Jesus. What is more, he had the skills in writing and probably also in shorthand, which was well known in antiquity. So, once again, we are brought back to bedrock, eyewitness testimony.

Luke wrote his gospel at much the same time, it seems, in the early eighties (though some people think he penned it nearly twenty years earlier). He was not a Jew, and he wrote especially for the benefit of non-Jews who were becoming Christians. He was not one of the original disciples of Jesus, but he tells us at the outset of his gospel that he had made extensive researches among those who were. It is evident that Mark's gospel and Matthew's sayings-source were among the primary materials that he examined and made good use of. The stories of the birth of Jesus and His early years were probably elicited from His mother Mary herself, and Luke's account of the resurrection of Jesus seems to have come from eyewitnesses, too. Luke has a particular gift for recounting the parables of Jesus: all the most memorable ones come in his gospel. He also has a profound care for the outcast, the helpless, the women, and the under-privileged. But perhaps his greatest achievement is to see the story of Jesus as only Part One of the continuing story of the church. His Acts of the Apostles is a deliberate continuation of the story of Jesus, and it is invaluable because it is the only one we have.

The most mysterious and majestic of all the Gospels is that ascribed to John. He was the most intimate friend of Jesus, a man with a strong mystical streak in him, and he contributes a striking, fresh perspective on the life and ministry of Jesus. And yet it is undeniably the same Jesus as the others describe. It is just that John seems to have gotten inside the mind of Jesus as no one else did. The actual authorship of this wonderful gospel has long been debated. It is now certain that it was either penned by the apostle John himself or written by a close disciple of his at John's direction. Some people think John's gospel was written before the fall of Jerusalem in A.D. 70, but most scholars agree with the Christians of the second century in seeing it as the last of the Gospels to be written, in the eighties when the apostle was an old man shepherding the church in Asia.

Such, in brief, are the Gospels. They were written between A.D. 65 and 85, and they are all anonymous (though the early Christians tell us who their authors were believed to be). This anonymity is not a weakness; it is rather a strength. All these Gospels reflect the joyful conviction of the whole Christian community that the Jesus who walked the streets of Galilee had conquered death and was calling people everywhere to come and follow Him. The Gospels are, if you like, the tip of the iceberg of faith, a tip that belongs to the great body of early believers hidden beneath the surface.

But questions crowd the mind...

Why So Comparatively Late?

For one thing, why were these Gospels written so comparatively long after the events they describe? For two reasons, both rather unfamiliar to us. In the first place, the early Christians were so busy preaching their good news all over the world that they would have been slow to think of writing it down. They were precipitating a religious movement that spread at an astonishing speed. Their priority was not writing books but making disciples.

The second reason is that ancient people preferred the spoken word to the written. Books were for those who had poor memories. And the ancient world prided itself on its memory. This holds true for the Greco-Roman world and the Jewish world alike. And in any case, book production was laborious and expensive before the days of printing. It was not something to tangle with unless you had to. By the sixties of the first century the Christians felt they had to. The generation of eyewitnesses was beginning to die off. The precious content of what they had to tell must be preserved.

Why Four Gospels?

Very well, but why *four* Gospels? Surely one would suffice? Interestingly enough, Christians in the second century asked that very same question and came up with an answer that satisfied them but will scarcely satisfy us. They said, "Of course there must be four Gospels. There are four seasons, four points on the compass; naturally there are four Gospels!" The straight answer is that we do not know. Just four Gospels emerged from the heart of the earliest church, and these are they. We can be very thankful that there were several accounts. For when you have multiple perspectives on a person or an event, it gives you a much more in-depth understanding. I for one am thankful for the diversity of the Gospels and the concerns of each individual evangelist. Such minor contradictions as they may contain (and even these are not proven) bother me not one whit. We do not have four photographs of Jesus: we have four portraits. Together they provide a depth of focus to our vision of Him that could never have been provided by a single version.

Has the Text Been Tampered With?

Do we have these Gospels as they were written? Or has the text been tampered with through the intervening centuries? Fortunately, we are in a position to give a very crisp answer to that question. No ancient documents in the whole world come down to us with such a wealth of manuscript tradition as the Gospels. We have copies of them going back to well within a century of their composition, and that is fantastic compared with classical authors of the period. The gap, for example, between when Tacitus wrote (some fifty years after the evangelists) and the earliest surviving manuscript of his work is eight hundred years. With Livy the historian, a contemporary of the evangelists, the gap is eleven hundred years. In striking contrast with the two or three manuscripts we have attesting the text of these secular writers, we have literally hundreds of the New Testament. They are written in many languages, and they come from all over the ancient world. They give us the text of the New Testament with astonishing uniformity. Of course, there are many variant readings in this vast array of manuscripts. But all who have studied the subject would agree on these two central points. First, no single doctrine of the New Testament depends on a disputed reading. Second, the text of the New Testament is so certain that no competent scholar would dream of making conjectural emendations (i.e., guesses about what the text should read), common though that is with the classical texts. The strength of the manuscript evidence makes such a procedure impossible.

Yes, we have the New Testament at large and the Gospels in particular as they were written. In all the Gospels there are only a couple of serious queries on the text. The first is whether Mark 16:9–20 was written by the evangelist or added by some of his friends to a gospel that looked unfinished. The other is whether the story of Jesus with the woman caught in adultery fits where it is normally placed in John 7:53 — 8:11 or where some manuscripts have it, after Luke 21:38.

Our four Gospels come to us with massive and continuous support over the centuries. There is every reason for confidence that we have them almost precisely as they left the hands of their authors.

Can We Trust What They Say?

"Ah," you may say, "but can we trust what they say?" That is the crunch issue. They make such astounding claims for Jesus and tell such amazing stories about Him. Can we believe them? That, of course, is a question on which you must make up your own mind. But there are very good reasons for trusting what those evangelists have to tell us.

First, no books in all the world's literature have been subjected to such thorough and persistent scrutiny over a period of hundreds of years as the Gospels. Today their credibility stands as high as ever. They emerge from every test with the utmost credit. That is an excellent reason for taking with the utmost seriousness the portrait they offer us of Jesus.

Second, there is a remarkable harmony in the picture they present. This is not only the case between the Gospels themselves but between them and the pattern of the early preaching as we learn it from Acts and from traces in other parts of the New Testament. There can be little doubt that such unplanned harmony among authors who were not colluding gives us the utmost confidence in the report they give us. These gospel writers were not making it up. They were telling us what happened.

Third, what we read in the Gospels fits closely with the secular evidence at which we have already glanced. But, of course, it fills it in and puts flesh on it. What is more, it chimes in precisely with what Paul, the great apostle, tells us in his scattered references to the historical Jesus. Paul wrote in the fifties and early sixties, probably a decade before the earliest of the Gospels. And his allusions are all the more impressive because they are so casual. He is not trying to prove anything or teach his readers something new about Jesus. He is simply reminding them of what they heard when they first became Christian disciples some years earlier. It would hardly be possible to have better or earlier supporting evidence for the trustworthiness of the Gospels.

Fourth, the survival of eyewitnesses of Jesus' ministry is an important factor to bear in mind when we are assessing the reliability of the Gospels. If the gospel writers were telling exaggerated stories about what Jesus did and said, there were still plenty of people around at the time of their publication who could have pointed out the errors. And in that case the Gospels simply would not have gained universal circulation and credit. But the eyewitnesses could not fault them, and they took off.

There are other ways of checking the trustworthiness of these remarkable little books. If the church had cooked up the contents of the Gospels, we should have expected them to put into Jesus' mouth statements about matters of burning concern to themselves. On the contrary we find that these issues (such as the lordship of Jesus, the Holy Spirit and His gifts, the controversy over the importance of circumcision, and whether Christians could eat food that had been offered to idols) are conspicuous by their absence. It gives us a great deal of confidence that the gospel writers were recording things that were true and not making things up that were convenient.

The parables provide another very interesting insight into the reliability of the gospel writers. People sometimes wonder whether these parables go back to Jesus Himself or whether the early Christians made them up. But why should anyone have pretended that Jesus taught in this remarkable way if He did not? Who could have been the genius to create them if not He? One thing is very clear. Nobody in Judaism before Him taught in parables like His. And nobody after Him was able to do so either. The members of the early church did not preach in parables; but they knew, and faithfully recorded, that Jesus had done so.

There are two critical tools of which the New Testament scholars are rightly fond. One they call the "criterion of multiple attestation." It simply means that there is added reason to accept the authenticity of some event or saying if it is recorded in more than one strand of the gospel tradition. Very well, apply that to the astounding story of Jesus' feeding of the five thousand from a few rolls and sardines. It sounds highly improbable, does it not?

Yet it is recorded in all four Gospels. You could not have more impeccable evidence than that. It is not the evidence that is at issue but whether we will believe the evidence.

The other tool is the matter of Aramaic. This was the language of Palestine in Jesus' day. It is the language Jesus generally spoke, though He was at least bilingual if not multilingual. Our Aramaic experts have discovered a remarkable thing. Much of the teaching of Jesus can easily be translated back into the underlying Aramaic, and when it is, it falls into rhyming cadences. This is very rare and very beautiful. It is also very memorable. That may account for the close verbal similarity, even identity, which we find in much of Jesus' teaching recorded in different Gospels. Jews learned by memorizing, and this rhyming Aramaic that underlies parts of our Gospels (and occasionally peeps out in words like *talitha cumi* and *abba*) is highly memorable. No doubt Jesus taught in this way because He wanted His teaching to be carefully remembered and accurately passed on. We have every reason to believe it was.

Conclusion

These are some of the grounds for relying on the truthfulness of the account the Gospels gave us of Jesus, astounding though that account undoubtedly is. As we have seen, the gospel evidence is very early. It comes from the first disciples. It ties in with the picture of Jesus we find roughly sketched by the secular sources, and it fits with the Jewish customs of the time. Scratch a gospel and you hit the underlying Aramaic, a sure sign that you are very near the actual words and deeds of Jesus in His own mother tongue. We have seen how the Gospels complement one another. We have seen that the text is so certain that there is no question of its having been tampered with down through the centuries. It is interesting that our modern secular historians generally give the highest regard to the testimony of the Gospels. These are all valid reasons for our confidence in the picture the Gospels give us.

But there is, I think, one overwhelming reason why we should believe the picture of Jesus given us in the Gospels. *Who could have made that picture up?* It reveals a Man so different from any other in the world, so sublime, so unexpected. Just suppose you and three friends were to sit down and write your impressions of the ideal human being. They would be sure to be very diverse. But the impressions of Jesus that the four evangelists record are remarkably harmonious. They are clearly portraits of the same person, displaying the same ideals, revealing the same character, giving the same teaching, and making the same claims. These men were writing fact, not fiction. They were trying to give an honest account of Jesus, the Man who made such an indelible impression on them all. And they were trying to nudge their readers into deciding for or against this Jesus as they read of His person, His offer, and His challenge. Therein lies their unchanging power.